W9-ANH-858

SHIFTING WORLD

SHIFTING WORLD

*Social Change and Nostalgia
in the American Novel*

David C. Stineback

Lewisburg
Bucknell University Press
London: Associated University Presses

Associated University Presses, Inc.
Cranbury, New Jersey 08512

Associated University Presses
108 New Bond Street
London W1Y OQX, England

Burgess

PS
374
·S67
S7

Library of Congress Cataloging in Publication Data
Stineback, David C. 1943-
Shifting World.

Bibliography: p.
Includes index.
1. American fiction—History and criticism.
2. Social change in literature. I. Title.
PS374.S67S7   813'.03   74-31510
ISBN 0-8387-1686-5

Earlier versions of chapters 6 and 10 appeared in *Arizona Quarterly* 29
(1973) and *Western American Literature* 6 (1971).

PRINTED IN THE UNITED STATES OF AMERICA

To
Ellen Gill
the source of whatever wisdom
this book contains

Contents

Acknowledgments

I began writing *Shifting World: Social Change and Nostalgia in the American Novel* eight years ago. Its research has been my own, but its inspiration belongs to others. I credit my wife, Ellen, with the book's underlying sense of historical change, the acceptance of which leads to the only authentic feeling of personal freedom and responsibility in Anglo-American culture. And I thank A. N. Kaul, now chairman of the English Department at the University of Delhi, India, for his faith in the accessibility of great literature to less than great minds. His conviction that characterization is the hallmark of the novel and that common sense is the key to appreciating characterization is apparent in this book.

For permission to quote from published works, I wish to thank the following publishers and organizations:

Doubleday & Co., Inc., for permission to quote from Richard Chase, *The American Novel and Its Tradition,* 1957. Reprinted by permission of the publisher, Doubleday & Co., Inc.

Harcourt, Brace, Jovanovich, Inc., for permission to quote from Ellen Glasgow, *The Sheltered Life,* originally

9

published by Doubleday, Doran, 1934. (Quoted by permission of the Richmond Society for the Prevention of Cruelty to Animals, whom I thank, also.)

Houghton Mifflin Co., and Brandt & Brandt, Inc., for permission to quote from A. B. Guthrie, Jr., *These Thousand Hills,* 1956. Reprinted by permission of the publisher, Houghton Mifflin Co.

G. P. Putnam's Sons, for permission to quote from Allen Tate, *The Fathers,* 1938.

Random House, Inc., for permission to quote from Willa Cather, *The Professor's House,* 1925, and William Faulkner, *The Hamlet,* 1940.

Introduction:
The Sense of the Sense of the Past

In a recent and very perceptive article on the sense of time found in the novel, Eleanor Hutchens says that "the reader who includes in his idea of the novel the experience of reading it . . . knows that at the core of that experience is the sense of moving through time that gradually shapes Emma's fate [in Flaubert's *Madame Bovary*] by a series of collisions with her will." A novel can do what a short story, a play, or a film can not adequately do, that is, "give us the fundamental conviction that its subjects have their origin, existence, and destiny in time."[1] If this is true of the novel, regardless of its period and place of composition, then I would suggest that it is one of the more interesting bibliographical facts in American literary history that most of the novels discussed in the following pages have received much less critical attention than they deserve and have never been discussed together, despite their marked similarities. They all present a situation of rapid social change in which the reader's own sense of time passing is accentuated by the histori-cal consciousness of the central character in each book. This would seem to be a particularly American phenomenon in fiction, as well as a particularly American reading experience. Yet the fact of rapid social change in America, so often com-mented upon by the most articulate observers from William Bradford to de Tocqueville and Charles Dickens,[2] hasn't had a very apparent impact on American fiction, as Richard Chase and other critics have shown.

11

Many factors could account for this discrepancy, but one significant one may be the degree to which the impermanence of American society gave some observers a curious feeling of sameness. A passage from de Tocqueville suggests this paradox:

> Fortunes, opinions, and laws are there in ceaseless variation; it is as if immutable Nature herself were mutable, such are the changes worked upon her by the hand of man. Yet in the end the spectacle of this excited community becomes monotonous, and after having watched the moving pageant for a time, the spectator is tired of it.
>
> Among aristocratic nations every man is pretty nearly stationary in his own sphere, but men are astonishingly unlike each other; their passions, their notions, their habits, and their tastes are essentially different; nothing changes, but everything differs. In democracies, on the contrary, all men are alike and do things pretty nearly alike. It is true that they are subject to great and frequent vicissitudes, but as the same events of good or adverse fortune are continually recurring, only the name of the actors is changed, the piece is always the same. The aspect of American society is animated because men and things are always changing, but it is monotonous because all these changes are alike.[3]

It may well have been this sameness of condition in which, nevertheless, "men and things are always changing" that prompted the American novelist's complaint about the "poverty of materials" available to the artist in America. But whatever their basis, the now familiar comments of Cooper, Hawthorne, and James on the absence of an adequate national history or social complexity to stimulate the novelist in America have led directly to the aforementioned argument of Richard Chase, Lionel Trilling, and Marius Bewley, among others, that American novelists have had a lack of interest in "the idea of society itself"[4] because there was "no social surface responsive to [their] touch."[5]

A few critics have sought to challenge these widely held and at times rather chauvinistic assumptions.[6] In "Mass Society and Post-Modern Fiction," Irving Howe merely questioned, in passing, the conclusion "that the presumed absence in recent years of a fixed, stratified society or of what one critic, with enviable naiveté, calls 'an agreed picture of the universe' makes it impossible to study closely our social life, or to develop (outside of the South) human personalities rooted in a sense of tradition, or to write good novels dealing with social manners and relationships." These things can be done, Howe said, "simply because they have been done."[7] Thus, even if we acknowledge the validity of Trilling's observation that in America "our class struggle has been extraordinarily fluid" and that "our various upper classes have seldom been able or stable enough to establish their culture as authoritative,"[8] we are still left, historically, with a very real social context in which, to quote de Tocqueville once more, "new families are constantly springing up, others are constantly falling away, and all that remain change their condition; the woof of time is every instant broken and the track of generations effaced."[9]

The American novelist has indeed dealt, repeatedly if not predominantly, with just such a context, and the ten novels discussed in the following chapters indicate the thrust of that effort. I've chosen these novels not only to represent ten different authors, but also to indicate the extent to which each is either 1) a departure, in the cases of Cooper, Hawthorne, Wharton, Cather, Glasgow, Faulkner, and Guthrie, from the dominant "romantic" or "naturalistic" concerns of the author's other major works, or 2) a very much ignored or underrated work (*The Pioneers, Democracy, The Bostonians, The Professor's House,* and *The Fathers*). Together they reflect a frank recognition of rapid social change as a fact of life in American society. In this sense "the piece is always the same," in de Tocqueville's phrase, though the locus of the drama, again by my choice, is slightly different in each work. For the author of *The Pioneers,* the reflector of social change is Nature, while, in *The House of the Seven Gables,* it is history and "the track of generations." In *Democracy,* it is politics; in *The Bostonians,* social reform; in *The House of Mirth,* social competition; in *The Professor's House,* religion and art; in *The Sheltered Life,* marriage and the family; in *The Fathers,* war; and in *The Hamlet,* business. Finally, in A. B. Guthrie, Jr.'s *These Thousand Hills,* the reader returns again to the frontier and Nature, but this time the author is concerned with the growth of the pioneer settlement rather than its origin. Regardless of its specific context and form, however, the presence of rapid social change in these novels is their common denominator and is quite objectively equated by their authors with the irreversible course of American history. These are, in effect, novels *about* history.

Certainly many other American novels besides these deal directly with the processes of history. Works like *The Great Gatsby, Absalom, Absalom!,* or, more recently, Evan Connell's *Mrs. Bridge* treat the fact of social change as a private crisis of experience or age, even if that private crisis has a larger, metaphorical significance. Gatsby, for example, has embarked on a personal quest that reflects his obliviousness to history and its effects, though he remains its inevitable victim; thanks to his innocence, he seems out of place in his own time, and his predicament, therefore, takes on mythic proportions. In a different vein, other American novelists have dramatized history in the form of what might be called *the family epic,* in which the author's focus often transcends the crises of individual generations and suggests the survival of shared values. Witness Conrad Richter's trilogy (*The Trees, The Fields, The Town*), Glenway Wescott's *The Grandmothers,* or Eudora Welty's novels. In such situations, within a family context, social change frequently loses some of its sting.

But in contrast to these versions of social change and the passage of time, the American novels discussed in the following pages concentrate on the individual's recognition of and reaction to history as an irresistible, ongoing process of loss and disappointment. To borrow a statement from Henry James, the central characters in these novels "are interesting only in proportion as they feel their respective situations; since the consciousness, on their part, of the complication exhibited forms for us their link of connection with it."[10] In each of these works, the "complication exhibited" is a rapidly changing physical and social environment, but the actual drama of the novels resides in the individual's "consciousness" of that complication.[11] At times, it is less a question of consciousness in the Jamesian sense than simply a habitual, almost instinctive fear of disorder; but, in either case, the individual is responding to the incoherence of his social situation. What Carl Jung considered the spiritual problem of modern man—"the yearning for rest that arises in a period of unrest"[12]—is precisely the dilemma of Natty Bumppo, the Pyncheons, Mrs. Lee, Basil Ransom and Olive Chancellor, Lily Bart, Professor St. Peter, George Posey, Lat Evans, and the inhabitants of Washington Street and Frenchman's Bend. In their separate historical situations and in differing degrees, these characters suffer from, in Jung's phrase, an "enormous tension . . . between objective and subjective reality,"[13] to the point where their subjective response to objective reality becomes the crux of their characters.

To be more specific, the individual character's "yearning for rest"[14] (or, more accurately, for stability) frequently takes the form of nostalgia for the past and, in particular, an insistent sense that the present is somehow morally or spiritually inferior to an earlier period in history. Madeleine Lee chooses to believe that, in a simpler, more heroic past, "everything Washington touched, he purified" and that Senator Ratcliffe's present willingness to accept "the good and the bad together" is a symptom of America's moral decline.[15] Basil Ransom unequivocally decides that, in contrast to an earlier age of elegance and chivalry, the society of post-Civil War America and Boston in particular has become too "talkative, querulous, hysterical, maudlin, full of false ideas, of unhealthy germs, of extravagant, dissipated habits, for which a great reckoning was in store."[16] Disturbed by the material ambitions and personal opportunism of his twentieth-century environment, Professor St. Peter longs for the "immortal repose" of an ancient Indian civilization in the Southwest; and the Archbalds attempt to preserve a "sheltered" antebellum style of life amidst the new attitudes and methods of science and industry.

One could cite many other examples from these novels of characters who resist the present by willingly or unwillingly clinging to the forms and values of the past. But what is finally most important is not *what* these characters believe, but *how* they believe; that is, the degree to which their beliefs prevent them from "let[ting] the past disappear," in Ellen Glasgow's words, and "hold[ing] firmly to the bare structure of living."[17] Even though the author may seem to share, at times, the nostalgia of his or her characters in these novels (Cooper, Adams, Wharton, Cather, Glasgow, and Faulkner are the most obvious examples), it is nonetheless clear that the novelist, in these situations, almost invariably perceives the illusions with which his most sympathetic characters attempt to confront the historical realities of American society. Thus Henry James can agree with Basil Ransom that something "heroic" has gone out of American life in the social chaos that followed the Civil War, while, at the same time, he can interpret this situation as a sad but inevitable historical development rather than a remediable moral decline. And we are left with the irony of the novel's conclusion in which Ransom's self-styled "victory" over Olive Chancellor is surely one of the most Pyrrhic in all of American literature.

Irony, in fact, is the single narrative and structural device that most clearly unites the novels discussed at length in the following pages. And Andrew Wright's definition of irony as "the juxtaposition of two mutually incompatible views of life" is particularly useful here. The ironist, Wright says, is characterized "by his recognition of the antitheses in human experience: his is an interested objectivity; he is detached but not indifferent, withdrawn but not removed."[18] Within these limits the novelist can deal with tragic ironies, comic ironies, or any other forms of irony that fall between these two. Certainly Wright's definition applies equally to Captain Ahab's death and to Huck Finn's self-condemnation in the language of Miss Watson. Furthermore, the evidence of American literature would seem to indicate that the tragic and comic forms of irony have a very similar structure: both deal with conflicts in human experience that are virtually irreconcilable and in which the individual is usually at the mercy of a greater, impersonal power, in the form of divine justice, fate, society, and so forth. The irony of the individual's situation is tragic or comic depending on the cost, in body and spirit, that that power exacts from him. The two novels in the present study, for example, that come closest to visions of tragic irony (*The House of Mirth*) and comic irony (*The Hamlet*) both concern the irresistible exploitation of naiveté and innocence by more powerful economic forces; in the former, Lily Bart's unsuspiciousness and generosity leads to poverty and death, but, in the latter, Faulkner's villagers are merely cajoled and blackmailed into a helpless sacrifice of their own economic and social power. In either case, whether comic or tragic, the conclusion seems foregone.

Those forms of irony that fall somewhere in between tragedy and comedy tend, on the other hand, to present antitheses in human experience that are potentially reconcilable without at least the loss of the individual's ability to function within his society. This is basically true of the ten novels discussed here and of *Don Quixote,* which Wright uses to illustrate his general definition of irony. By keeping the duality of his own sympathies in equilibrium, Cervantes repeatedly forces the reader to applaud the nobility of Don Quixote's sentiments and, at the same time, to censure the hero's "arrant foolishness" and "inadequacy of judgment."[19] Similarly, the question of reality and illusion—in terms of social change and nostalgia for the past—is central to those American novels whose ironies, in the last analysis, generate something like pathos rather than the emotions of tragedy. Works such as Henry Adams's *Democracy,* Willa Cather's *The Professor's House,* and Ellen Glasgow's *The Sheltered Life* assume a fundamental reality of historical change and disappointment, in the face of which the sensitive individual is sorely tempted to find personal solace in an illusory contrast between present corruption and past virtue. For the authors themselves, however, much as they sympathize with the illusions of their characters, the greatest virtues are self-knowledge and resignation. Their irony, therefore, is reserved primarily for those "heroes" and "heroines" who, because of their own restlessness and insecurity, tend to overestimate the past or choose to judge negatively the processes of historical change. Whether in the form of Mrs. Lee's "bolts of divine justice," Basil Ransom's righteous conservatism, Lily Bart's and St. Peter's "passion for the appropriate," or the inflexible community rituals of Washington Street and Frenchman's Bend, the recourse to moralism, these authors are saying, can not cope with the amoral realities of history; to act as if it could is to deceive oneself. Thus, the novels discussed here are not only *about history,* but about the need to *be realistic* about history.

By clinging to established habits or chosen illusions in opposition to the actuality of social change, the alienated and nostalgic characters in these novels frequently become as inflexible in their thinking as if they were, in fact, members of a more stable, less democratic social order, or the protagonists in a classic novel of manners by Jane Austen or W. M. Thackeray. Through them, their authors attest to the ironic fact that, in a democracy, the very absence of traditional codes and manners may produce, in certain individuals, an "aristocratic" manner of thought and behavior.

This is the American novelist's vision of one stage in the process of social change—the stage at which the individual is capable of remembering or imagining a time when men were, or at least seemed, in control of their environment. To be thus preoccupied with the past is alien to a historical period in which, according to Nicholas Berdyaev, "the human spirit has been wholly and organically contained in some fully crystallized, fully matured and settled epoch."[20] Rather, an urgent sense of history grows out of a "disruption . . . in man's historical life and conscience"—a phrase reminiscent of the "restlessness in the midst of prosperity" that de Tocqueville considered typical of democracies.[21] And if this idea of disruption can be applied to the nature of American society, then it may help to explain the provincialism that Cooper called "the governing social evil of America." He complained that

without a social capital, with twenty or more communities divided by distance and political barriers, her people, who are really more homogeneous than any other of the same numbers in the world perhaps, possess no standard for opinion, manners, social maxims, or even language. Every man, as a matter of course, refers to his own particular experience, and praises or condemns the notions contracted in the circle of his own habits, however narrow, provincial, or erroneous they may happen to be.[22]

In this sense, the nostalgic characters in the novels discussed here represent only one form of democratic provincialism, though its most ironic form. Their longing for the permanence, coherence, and moral security of a stable social community may be admirable in its refinement and taste, but any search for a "standard for opinion" and established "manners" in a democracy is futile. The more aristocratic one is in spirit, the more one must learn, like Professor St. Peter, "to live without delight."

Certainly by his own definition, James Fenimore Cooper became a provincial himself, particularly in his later works; and there is no reason to assume that any of the authors of these American novels have been less susceptible than their characters to the "disruption [of] historical life and conscience" and to the nostalgic provincialism that is often its consequence. Still, though they may at times share with their characters the longing for a previously "crystallized," "matured," and "settled" period in history, they have been able, in varying degrees, to transcend their initial experience of what Berdyaev called "spiritual dismemberment." The result, again, is an attitude of ironic detachment in their work that comes with an understanding and expression of history as an irreversible process of change. While the American novelist may indeed have had, as Hawthorne asserted, "no shadow, no antiquity, no mystery, no picturesque and gloomy wrong, nor anything but a commonplace prosperity" to work with,[23] what he did have, if these ten novels are any indication, was an astute sense of historical change and of the psychological perils of a "commonplace prosperity" in a democratic society—an awareness, in other words, of the anxieties suffered by the individual who hopelessly desires the social security of an established system of habits and manners. Perhaps the most appropriate phrase for this awareness is the quality that T.

S. Eliot attributed to Henry James: the sense of the sense of the past.[24]

In the novels discussed in the following pages, that "sense" has led to an understanding both of the processes of history and of the emotional burdens that those processes entail. Change in the present and nostalgia for the past are the antagonists here; and their conflict, in the American novel, has been, like American history itself, irrepressible.

SHIFTING WORLD

1

"This comes of settling a country!": James Fenimore Cooper's *The Pioneers*

During his career, James Fenimore Cooper often complained of the "poverty" of the materials available to the novelist in America. "All that glow," he concluded in his third preface to *The Spy,* "which can be given to a tale through the aid of obscure legends, artificial distinctions, and images connected with the association of ideas, is not attainable in this land of facts."[1] Similarly, in his preface to *Home as Found,* Cooper declared that

> this country, in its ordinary aspects, probably presents as barren a field to the writer of fiction, and to the dramatist, as any other on earth; we are not certain that we might not say the most barren. . . . It would be indeed a desperate undertaking, to think of making anything interesting in the way of a *Roman de Société* in this country.[2]

And earlier, in *Notions of the Americans,* he expressed the same conviction at greater length:

> There is scarcely an ore which contributes to the wealth of the author, that is found, here, in veins as rich as in Europe. There are no annals for the historian; no follies (beyond the most vulgar and commonplace) for the satirist; no manners

23

for the dramatist; no obscure fictions for the writer of romance; no gross and hardy offences against decorum for the moralist; nor any of the rich artificial auxiliaries of poetry.[3]

By 1845, however, when he wrote *Satanstoe,* the first of the Littlepage trilogy, Cooper evidently felt he had found the "annals" he was looking for; there, in his Preface, he described himself as a "historian" and his novel as a "chronicle of manners."[4] The "drama" of *Satanstoe* is indeed concerned with the "gross and hardy offences against decorum" (in this case, against landed property in upstate New York) that Cooper attributed to the pre-Revolutionary ancestors of the nineteenth-century antirenters.

Satanstoe deserves mention only because it is the best of Cooper's acknowledged "novels of manners" and is typical of the kind of social novel one normally associates with Cooper. It would be wrong, however, to assume that Cooper never wrote a *Roman de Société* prior to the 1840s simply because he never acknowledged it as such. Perhaps the "glow" he was looking for was not to be found in the social scene of his own times; yet it would seem that none of Cooper's novels, including *Satanstoe,* deals more with the nature of American society than does *The Pioneers.* Published in 1823, it is the first of the Leatherstocking Tales and the first novel written exclusively, in Cooper's words, "to please myself." In the main, it contains none of the "obscure fictions" that Cooper considered the essential material of the romance writer. He probably realized this himself when he admitted, rather apologetically, that "happier periods, more interesting events, and, possibly, more beauteous scenes, might have been selected to exemplify my subject."[5] Instead, he turned to the "land of facts" before him and created, in the estimate of one critic, "a straightforward realistic novel, immensely rewarding at the level of the literal surface."[6]

The Pioneers is distinctive in the context of Cooper's other major works. As Donald Davie has pointed out, "it does not have that aura of myth which was in the later novels to gather so goldenly about the figure of Leatherstocking."[7] Taken together, *The Pioneers, The Last of the Mohicans, The Prairie, The Pathfinder,* and *The Deerslayer* can be and have been interpreted as Cooper's "romance" about the "myth of America"—the New World's dream of emancipating its spirit from the Old. But, while it is perfectly valid to read the entire Leatherstocking series as a single romance, one should also do justice to the changing nature of Cooper's imagination, to the changing character of Natty Bumppo, and to the individual status of a novel such as *The Pioneers*. Even granting Lawrence's claim that the Leatherstocking novels in their entirety are an expression of Cooper's "wish-fulfillment" and "an evasion of actuality,"[8] this does not necessarily mean that each of these tales "evades" reality in the same way or to the same degree. The very least one can say about the Leatherstocking tales that follow *The Pioneers* is that they reflect, in Lawrence's words, a "decrescendo of reality"[9] and an increase of "more beauteous scenes," to borrow Cooper's own phrase.

Put another way, the later Leatherstocking novels are more casuistical than *The Pioneers;* in them, as Davie has argued, Natty is often "placed in a situation where the conflict of loyalties is such as at all points to raise some very nice questions of morality."[10] This is especially true of *The Deerslayer*. While Hurry Harry and Tom Hutter are no different, in their rapacity and depredation, from Billy Kirby and Richard Jones in *The Pioneers,* their very survival in the wilderness, in contrast to Kirby's or Jones's, is largely dependent upon their obedience to Natty's own moral code. Isolated on the houseboat and surrounded by Indians, they would do well to listen to Natty's advice, for practical if not for moral reasons:

> I look upon the redmen to be quite as human as we are ourselves, Hurry. They have their gifts, and their religion, it's true; but that makes no difference in the end, when each will be judged according to his deeds, and not according to his skin.[11]

Whereas in *The Pioneers* Natty becomes the prisoner of man-made laws and institutions, in *The Deerslayer* it is Hurry Harry and the Hutters who are, in effect, the prisoners of Natty's legalism ("there is a law and a law-maker, that rule across the whole continent" [p. 15]) and of his constant 'sententiousness. Because March and Hutter have "lost their sense of natural devotion in lives of obdurate and narrow selfishness" (p. 332) and are motivated solely by a "heartless longing for profit" (p. 266), they are therefore subject to Natty's frequent sermons on the "nat'ral gifts" of Indians and "the whole 'arth" as "the temple of the Lord to such as have the right mind" (p. 269). And since the bounty hunters are not of a "right mind," they must suffer the consequences of their avarice. Thus, Tom Hutter's scalping is intended to be a fitting punishment "for his own recent attempts on the Iroquois," according to "the decrees of a retributive Providence" (p. 366). What is casuistical about *The Deerslayer,* and, for that matter, about the later Littlepage trilogy as well, is Cooper's determination to dramatize the progress of history in moral terms: those who see Nature as a source of profit rather than a "temple" of worship invariably merit either actual misfortune or the personal scorn and sarcasm of the author.

In *The Deerslayer* the laws of Nature are viable and effective, but in *The Pioneers* this balance of power has been upset, and Natty's moral code is not sustained by "a retributive Providence." Significantly, the most fitting event in the first of the Leatherstocking tales is Chingachgook's death in the forest fire—the direct result of man's destructive *im*providence toward Nature: the inhabitants of Templeton had often acquired their timber and fuel from the area of the fire,

> in procuring which, it was their usage to take only the bodies of the trees, leaving the tops and branches to decay under the operations of the weather. Much of the hill was, consequently, covered with such light fuel, which, having been scorched under the sun for the last two months, was ignited with a touch. Indeed, in some cases, there did not appear to be any contact between the fire and these piles, but the flames seemed to dart from heap to heap, as the fabulous fire of the temple is represented to re-illumine its neglected lamp.[12]

The difference between Chingachgook's death and Tom Hutter's death in *The Deerslayer* is the difference between a historical irony and a moral irony; the guiding principle of the latter is retribution and of the former, necessity. Though Cooper's sympathies with the natural world are no less apparent in *The Pioneers,* the presentation of his subject is accomplished with less vengeance and more detachment. His profiteers are not pictured as ill-fated offenders against a supreme Lawmaker; rather, the larger, inevitable movements of history (as opposed to the individual villain) are given the final responsibility for man's "improvidence." While Hurry Harry and Tom Hutter in *The Deerslayer* or Ishmael Bush in *The Prairie* are cut off from the protection and approval of human society and therefore are dependent, whether they like it or not, on the wisdom and assistance of Natty Bumppo, Richard Jones and Billy Kirby in *The Pioneers* are the agents of a larger community that hardly requires Natty's presence, much less his aid. For all their "strong excitement that is produced by battles and murders,"[13] the later Leatherstocking novels are essentially philosophical-moral dramas conducted in a prescribed environment where what one believes has a direct effect on one's survival; the safety of the individual depends upon his strict obedience to those inhabitants of Nature who are privileged to understand her secrets. In *The Pioneers,* however, the presiding environment is social, not natural, and the health and happiness of the individual ceases to depend upon his attitudes toward Nature. This is just as true of Natty as it is of Richard Jones and the other inhabitants of Templeton.

Only in the later tales of a younger Natty Bumppo (when civilization, in effect, recedes from the wilderness) did Cooper attempt to re-create the once established relationship between Nature and his hero, which the reader of *The Pioneers* can only imagine. Perhaps one could argue that Cooper grew to fear the evolving democratic society that he embodied so skillfully in the village of Templeton and that he increasingly sought to depict, during the rest of his career, a subject that would reflect a form of natural or social stability. It is not the purpose of this discussion, however, to speculate on Cooper's own motives, nor to pass judgment on the worth of his earlier or later works. It is simply to record those characteristics that make *The Pioneers,* for better or worse, a distinctive creation for its author and for its time in the history of American literature.

More than in any of Cooper's other novels or in those of any other American novelist until William Faulkner, there is a profound sense in *The Pioneers* of Nature "rapidly altering under the hands of man" (p. 28). In the other Leatherstocking tales, change is merely suggested, presumed, or threatened as an almost intangible context for the immediate moral romance. But in *The Pioneers* it is the author's central concern. While Cooper describes the settling of upstate New York after the Revolutionary War as a "magical change" in "the power and condition of the state" (p. 3), the feeling of regret that comes through his description, for example, of the ruined trees in chapter 3 is a truer indication of his sympathies:

> Many a pile of snow [in Templeton] betrayed the presence of the stump of a pine; and even in one or two instances, unsightly remnants of trees that had been partly destroyed by fire were seen rearing their black, glistening columns twenty or thirty feet above the pure white of the snow. These, which in the language of the country are termed *stubs,* abounded in the open fields adjacent to the village, and were accompanied, occasionally, by the ruin of a pine or a hemlock that had been stripped of its bark, and which waved in melancholy grandeur its naked limbs to the blast, a skeleton of its former glory (p. 34).

"Five years," Cooper concludes somewhat nostalgically, "had wrought greater changes than a century would produce in older countries where time and labour have given permanency to the works of man" (p. 35).

In *The Deerslayer* and *The Prairie,* Natty Bumppo either has not yet encountered the full force of the westward movement in America or he has already fled from it; regardless, he finds the security he needs in a reflective, philosophical outlook on life, be it Christian or fatalistic. In *The Pioneers,* however, it is the permanency of Natty's own way of life in the wilderness that is most directly affected by the rapid settlement of Templeton. Consequently, Natty is on the defensive for the first and only time in the Leatherstocking Tales. After *The Pioneers,* he always controls his immediate environment, not vice versa. When Natty is introduced in the opening chapter, for instance, he reveals a degree of self-interest and anger that is missing from his portrayal in the later novels:

> "The game is becoming hard to find, indeed, Judge, with your clearings and betterments," said the old hunter, with a kind of compelled resignation. "The time has been, when I have shot thirteen deer, without counting the fa'ns, standing in the door of my own hut! and for bear's meat, if one wanted a ham or so, he had only to watch a-nights, and he could shoot one by moonlight, through the cracks of the logs" (p. 9).

Unlike the later Natty, Cooper's hero in *The Pioneers* is not simply a disinterested combatant and a spokesman for higher laws in the battle against man's depredation of Nature: the eventual philosophical drama has been postponed for the time being by a personal drama in which Natty's own survival is in question. "You didn't use to be so prutent," Major Hartmann tells him, "as to look ahet mit so much care." "Maybe there wasn't so much occasion," Natty replies. "I have lived to see what I thought eyes could never behold in these hills, and I have no heart left for singing" (pp. 158–59, 162).

The occasion Natty is referring to is paraphrased in the epigraph Cooper borrowed from James Kirke Paulding for the first edition of *The Pioneers:*

> Extremes of habits, manners, time and space,
> Brought close together, here stood face to face,
> And gave at once a contrast to the view,
> That other lands and ages never knew.

And the two most fundamental extremes in the novel are Natty and Judge Temple. Though in their opposition to the wasteful use of Nature the two men are in agreement, Marmaduke Temple's entire life has been dedicated to the "affluence and comfort that was expanding around him" (p. 35), while Natty would prevent even this use of Nature if he could. The former always devotes the fruits of his industry to social change; the latter always defends the permanence of the natural world. Unlike the Judge, Natty never loses sight of these basic differences: "We are not much of one mind," he tells the Judge, "or you'd never turn good hunting-grounds into stumpy pastures" (p. 272).

From Natty's point of view, no distinction can or should be made between the law of Judge Temple and the anarchy of Billy Kirby;[14] both are the products of a larger historical movement. As Natty tells Chingachgook, the wilderness would still be "a comfortable hunting-ground . . . but for the money of Marmaduke Temple, and the twisty ways of the law" (p. 299). Through the window of his own enterprise, the Judge sees Natty's resistance to the settlement as merely a personal opposition to "an innovation on his rights . . . to an interruption of the hunting" (p. 240). When Oliver Effingham raises the possibility that Natty might also be resisting "the justice of the tenure by which the whites hold the country" from the Indians, Judge Temple admits that Natty once spoke of this, but that he (the Judge)

> did not clearly comprehend him, and may have forgotten what [Natty] said; for the Indian title was extinguished so far back as the close of the old war; and if it had not been at all, I hold under the patents of the royal governors, confirmed by an act of our own State legislature, and no court in the country can affect my title (p. 241).

Thus, as long as it is protected by law, might makes right for Judge Temple as surely as it does for the more rapacious members of his community. Natty is probably correct: history and morality will be joined again only on "the great day when the whites shall meet the redskins in judgment, and justice shall be the law, and not power" (p. 476).[15]

There is no indication in *The Pioneers* that that day could ever come in their life. The only Indian portrayed by Cooper is Chingachgook, the last of the Mohicans. But Natty's friend is a far cry from the much much nobler savage of the later Leather-stocking novels. Thanks to the white man's poison and its antidote—rum and Christianity—the Indian has become a guilt-ridden drunk, lost in his nostalgic memories of past battles against the Mingos. "The white man brings old age with him," he tells Natty and Oliver, "rum is his tomahawk" (p. 185). But when the young hunter asks him why "one so noble, aid[s] the devices of the devil, by making himself a beast," Chingachgook can only respond with pathetic self-abasement:

> Yes; you say no lie, child of the Fire-eater! John is a beast. . . . My fathers came from the shores of the salt lake. They fled before rum. They came to their grandfather, and they lived in peace; or, when they did raise the hatchet, it was to strike it into the brain of a Mingo. They gathered around the council-fire, and what they said was done. Then John was the man. But warriors and traders with light eyes followed them. One brought the long knife, and one brought rum. They were more than the pines on the mountains; and they broke up the councils, and took the lands. The evil spirit was in their jugs, and they let him loose. Yes, yes—you say no lie, Young Eagle; John is a Christian beast (p. 185).

Still, the fact that Chingachgook has lost his self-control is not nearly as pathetic as his refusal to resist or even to condemn openly the white man's influence. When Oliver initially declines the Judge's offer of a home and job, the Indian puts on "the fearless and proud front of an Indian warrior" and says,

> Let the Young Eagle and the Great Land Chief eat together; let them sleep, without fear, near each other. The children of Miquon love not blood; they are just, and will do right. The sun must rise and set often, before men can make one family; it is not the work of a day, but of many winters. . . . Learn to wait, my son; you are a Delaware, and an Indian warrior knows how to be patient. . . . The Delaware warrior sits still, and waits the time of the Great Spirit. He is no woman, to cry out like a child (pp. 205, 208).

Cooper apparently wants his readers to admire this passive resignation in Chingachgook; if so, then he, too, has resigned himself to the idea that one must wait patiently, without judgment, for the time that God has ordained for justice, whether in this life or the next. It is one thing, however, to resign oneself to the injustices of history out of personal powerlessness, but it is quite another thing to resign oneself to history out of a baseless trust in its ultimate redemption. Cooper suggests both alternatives—in the characters of Natty and Chingachgook, respectively—but finally refuses to commit his sympathies to either vision.

Of course, the rediscovery and reimbursement of the Effingham family in *The Pioneers* is designed to prove that patience can be a virtue and some measure of justice can be achieved. Oliver Edwards is initially a more outspoken opponent of Judge Temple than either Natty or Chingachgook. Though he himself has no Indian blood, he is the grandson of the "rightful owner" (through an Indian gift after adoption into the tribe) of the property on which Marmaduke has built his town. Chingachgook's advice to be patient "seem[s] to have great weight with the young man" (p. 205), who consents to work and live with Judge Temple. Eventually Oliver's true identity as an Effingham is revealed, when the existence of his grandfather (who has been sheltered by Natty Bumppo, the old family servant) is disclosed, and he marries the Judge's daughter Elizabeth, finally inheriting the entire estate upon the deaths of her father and Major Effingham. Thus, the original will of the Indians is respected by the eventual owners of the land.

Yet, while this may prove that Marmaduke Temple is personally a "just" man, particularly toward those white men who entrusted him with their property, it can only be a secondhand victory for the Indians. The argument that Oliver Effingham's final inheritance represents the replacement of an "illegitimate" authority by a "legitimate" one with the "sanction of tradition" and "roots in the continuity of history" is tempting but misleading.[16] While such a resolution may be designed to give an orderly symbolic structure to the novel, Oliver Effingham's distinctly personal and passive opposition to the Judge, in contrast to the active moral opposition of Natty Bumppo, establishes

Oliver's own preoccupation with expediency and property. Morally, there can never be a rightful or "legitimate" owner of Indian land, only a more considerate one.

Yet, contrived and casuistical as it seems, the Effingham story does at least contribute, by its very lack of imagination, to an appreciation of the contradictions and ambiguities that prevail in *The Pioneers*. Without it, the sense of injustice that remains at the end of the novel might seem less significant, Cooper's own feelings of resignation toward the historical plight of the Indians less frustrating and problematical, and the final persistence and honesty of his vision of history, in the person of Natty Bumppo, less remarkable.

In the largest sense, Cooper's sympathies in *The Pioneers* are divided three ways among Judge Temple, Chingachgook, and Natty; but it is not the nature of history that is in question: "might makes right" has been its modus operandi. Rather, the question is how one should react to the injustice of this state of affairs. Though Temple himself may be a just man, the success of his settlement depends upon the energy of careless men like Richard Jones; and Marmaduke, as Cooper says after the fishing scene, "appeared to understand that all opposition to the will of the Sheriff would be useless" (p. 273). Whereas the Judge is inclined to resign himself to the role of the victor, Chingachgook passively acquiesces in his role as the victim. But Natty resists the forces of history (even as he understands them) until his own way of life is endangered, and he then moves farther west. It is difficult for the reader to sympathize with all three responses to history, as Cooper seems to wish.

The problem with the novel, in this respect, stems from the fact that Chingachgook, Natty Bumppo, and Judge Temple all represent, for Cooper, certain forms or stages of order, each of which elicits the author's own feelings of respect. In the last analysis, Cooper could not completely accept the idea of an inherent conflict between human society and Nature, between the chaos of history and the order of Creation, between social change and divine justice. He believed, for example, that "men of the same habits, the same degree of cultivation and refinement, the same opinions, *naturally associate together,* in every class of life"[17] (italics added), and that this, therefore, is the way things ought to be. Status is God-given and extends throughout society, in its most primitive stages as well as its most complex, and the "gentleman" of learning, taste, sentiment, and refinement stands at the apex of the natural order.[18] Thus, while Judge Temple may cause a great deal of change, it is solely in the name of a future stability for his society, after the necessary changes involved in settling the wilderness have run their course — an eventual "old country" run by a landed gentry with its "Mansion-houses" and "Squires," not unlike the system that Cooper defended in the Littlepage trilogy. "They who do not see and feel the importance," said Cooper, "of possessing a class of such men in a community, to give it tone, a high and far-sighted policy, and lofty views in general, can know little of history."[19] The democratic community may indeed need such men, but Cooper himself "knew" little of history in thinking that the kind of natural aristocracy that he admired could survive, historically, in America; and *The Pioneers* shows, indeed, that it could not.

In Chingachgook, Natty Bumppo, and Judge Temple, Cooper created three "gentlemen"—each having been or destined to be, within the structure of his own environment, a leading figure in an aristocracy. Of course, the irony is that each succeeding environment has displaced the previous one and, with it, the status and function of its leader. Alone among white men, the Christianized Chingachgook is lost in his memories of the "old days"; and Natty is, in one sense, only "the foremost in that band of pioneers who are opening the way for the march of our nation across the continent" (p. 477).

Cooper was probably aware of the historical conflicts built into his subject in *The Pioneers* and, fortunately, could not or did not suppress them. He did, however, try to ameliorate the situation by bringing all three of his gentlemen under the unifying umbrella of Christianity, as if what his characters professed to believe could alter the facts of their history. The trouble is that the historical function and conduct of the Christian church can contradict the faith and ideals of Christianity. Even though Natty, for example, believes that "the Lord . . . lives in clearings as well as in the wilderness" (p. 476), he still feels that the Church must bear some responsibility for the invasion and depredation of the wilderness:

> I never knowed preaching come into a settlement but it made game scearce, and raised the price of gun-powder; and that's a thing that's not as easily made as a ramrod or an Indian flint (p. 131).

Nor are the Moravians, who "Christianized" Chingachgook, inculpable: according to Natty, they

> were always overintimate with [Chingachgook's tribe]. It's my opinion that, had they been left to themselves, there would be no such doings now, about the head waters of the two rivers, and that these hills mought have been kept as good hunting-ground (p. 153).

Thus when Natty accompanies Chingachgook to the church service in chapter 11, Cooper says his "countenance expressed uneasiness" and "plainly indicated some unusual causes for unhappiness" (p. 128). Even the Indian, on occasion, can not restrain his bitterness toward the white man's supposedly Christian conduct. When Elizabeth patronizingly congratulates him for having "learned to fear God and to live at peace" after his tribe had disappeared, Chingachgook questions the settlers' own fear of God:

> Where are the blankets and merchandize that bought the right of the Fire-eater? are they with him in his wigwam? Did they say to him, Brother, sell us your land, and take this gold, this silver, these blankets, these rifles, or even this rum? No; they tore it from him, as a scalp is torn from an enemy; and they that did it looked not behind them, to see whether he lived or died. Do such men live in peace, and fear the Great Spirit? (p. 417).

And in a final moment of dignity Chingachgook resigns his soul at death to the "Great Spirit of the savages." Natty's epitaph is bitter: "Red skin or white, it's all over now! He's to be judged by a righteous Judge, and by no laws that's made to suit times, and new ways" (p. 441).

Cooper, however, attempts to moderate Natty's bitterness by insisting, with a curiously ironic metaphor, that "although the faith of the hunter was by no means clear, yet the fruits of early instruction had not entirely fallen in the wilderness. He believed in one God, and one heaven" (p. 439). By thus stressing the Christian tolerance and understanding of Natty Bumppo, Cooper can make the narrow denominationalism of Mr. Grant, the town preacher, appear almost comic rather that misguided or harmful. Similarly, in chapters 11 and 12, Cooper plays down the serious differences between Natty's and the preacher's attitudes toward the role of Christianity in history, and presents Mr. Grant as a somewhat benign and necessary figure in the future "civilization" of Templeton. These scenes and the ones that follow in the town tavern (chapters 13 and 14), in fact, are the best examples in *The Pioneers* of the uneasy division in Cooper's sympathies between the growing rigidity and exclusiveness of a Christian society, under the guidance of Judge Temple, and Natty's concern for the permanence of God's creation in Nature. And it is from these scenes—where the inhabitants of Templeton, along with Natty and Chingachgook, are assembled in the village's two most "democratic" structures, the church and the tavern—that one can best determine the truth or falsity of Cooper's contention that "the freedom of manners that prevailed in the new settlements, commonly levelled all difference in rank, and with it, frequently, all considerations of education and intelligence" (p. 411). Can the future order that Cooper envisions for Templeton actually accommodate those individuals whose own "aristocratic" relationship with Nature has been corrupted by historical change?

Chapter 11, for example, seems to be an attempt by Cooper to justify his earlier observation that, in the newly settled wilderness, "places for the public worship of God abound with that frequency which characterizes a moral and reflecting people, and with that variety of exterior and canonical government which flows from unfettered liberty of conscience" (p. 2). Of course, at the time of Cooper's story, Templeton has no actual churches and only one minister, who is Episcopalian. But it is clear from the "disputatiousness" of Mr. Grant's congregation, who "owed their very existence, as a distinct nation, to the doctrinal character of their ancestors" (p. 125), that there will indeed be in the near future a representative variety of Christian worship in Templeton. Though they have come from "half the nations in the north of Europe," the villagers are still "a primitive people in their habits," and, "being a good deal addicted to subtleties and nice distinctions in their religious opinions," they view "the introduction of any such temporal assistance as form into their spiritual worship, not only with jealousy, but [also] frequently with disgust" (p. 122). Thus confronted with the "ignorance" of his listeners, Mr. Grant skillfully steers a middle course between formal creeds and general morality. By insisting upon both the "feeling of universal philanthropy" and the need for a "form of evangelical discipline," the minister, in Cooper's words, "so happily blended the universally received opinions of the Christian faith with the dogmas of his own church, that, although none were entirely exempt from the influence of his reasons, very few took any alarm at the innovation" (p. 123). As Cooper portrays him, Mr. Grant is not just an Episcopalian minister: because of his long experience with "human nature," he is the orthodox patron of Templeton's religious future, and the leading sponsor of the "visible church" in its various forms.

Whether this will be a truly democratic future is another question. It will if democracy means the coexistence of many different denominations each with "its own distinctive precepts" (p. 122). But, together, these donominations will be united against all heresies that fail to "acknowledge the attributes of the Saviour, and depend on his mediation" (p. 125). Therefore, in chapter 12, Mr. Grant feels that Chingachgook's invocation of "the Great Spirit" is "a little heterodox," and is attracted, instead, to the "respectful and pious manner" of Oliver Edwards (p.129). "I am delighted to meet with you," the minister says, "for I think an ingenuous mind, such as I doubt not yours must be, will exhibit all the advantages of a settled doctrine and devout liturgy" (p. 133). Though Chingachgook has also been Christianized, Oliver has had the advantage of having been raised in a Christian society; it is a "civilized" education, according to Mr. Grant, "not colour, nor lineage, that constitutes merit; and I know not that he who claims affinity to the proper owners of this soil has not the best right to tread these hills with the lightest conscience" (p. 137). But "conscience, " unfortunately, is not the final measure of right and wrong for Mr. Grant; if it were, then Chingachgook would have an even better right than Oliver to "tread these hills." From the minister's point of view (and, at times, it would seem, from Cooper's as well), the white man's invasion and settlement of the wilderness has not been a question of "education" or "universal philanthropy" (as patronizing as that might be), but rather a question of racial (and therefore religious) superiority. Despite his disclaimer about "colour" and "lineage," for example, what is one to make of Mr. Grant's reaction to Oliver's scorn for Judge Temple: "It is the hereditary violence of a native's passion . . . He is mixed with the blood of the Indians, you have heard; and neither the refinements of education, nor the advantages of our excellent liturgy, have been able entirely to eradicate the evil" (p. 139)? And, when Louisa asks her father if there is any danger of Oliver's "relapsing into the worship of his ancestors," he replies that "his white blood would prevent it" (p. 140). Of course, the reader at this point suspects what the minister can not imagine, that Oliver actually has no Indian blood at all, so the racial prejudice of the minister's remarks is somewhat mitigated by the plot of the novel. Nevertheless, Mr. Grant's comments remain as a measure of his religion.

The following tavern scene in the Bold Dragoon seems to be an attempt by Cooper to moderate the tone of his preceding chapter (as if he felt that by creating a greater sympathy in the reader's mind for Natty and Chingachgook he could somehow complement his own sympathy for the "civilized" attitudes of Mr. Grant). Yet neither in its function nor its essence can the tavern really be distinguished from the church: one is the meeting place for "men of different occupations," while the other is the meeting place for people of different denominations. In the former scene, the "universally received opinions of the Christian faith" are delivered to the entire congregation; in the latter, "the liquor was passed from one to the other" (p. 145). And in both the tavern and the church the attitudes of the villagers are the same.

This time, however, Natty, too, is condemned by "a room full of Christian folks" (p. 147). Mrs. Hollister, the landlady, calls him "a poor hunter, who is but a little better in his ways than the wild savages themselves," and expresses the hope that "the missionaries will, in [Natty's] own time, make a convarsion of the poor divils" (p. 147). Natty himself then enters and assumes the same position he took during Mr. Grant's sermon—"on the end of one of the logs that lay nigh to the fires" (pp. 120, 150). When he eventually invokes his own religion of Nature and bemoans the scarcity of game in the woods, Major Hartmann responds with the single comment in *The Pioneers* that best summarizes the social and religious attitudes of Templeton, from the Judge and Mr. Grant down to shiftless Jotham Riddel: "Ter lant is not mate as for ter teer to live on, put for Christians" (p. 158). All the Christians in the Bold Dragoon can sing and get drunk on liquor as they might sing and get drunk, with more decorum, on their hymns in church, but for Natty, who is harboring the "rightful ruler" of the land, Major Effingham, in his cabin, "it ill becomes them that have lived by his bounty to be making merry, as if there was nothing in the world but sunshine and summer" (p. 162).

Chingachgook's presence in the Bold Dragoon only reaffirms Natty's point of view. Richard Jones jokingly dismisses the hunter's criticisms:

Merry! ay! merry Christmas to you, old boy! Sunshine and summer! no! you are blind, Leather-Stockin, 'tis moonshine and winter; take these spectacles, and open your eyes,—

"So let us be jolly,
And cast away folly,
For grief turns a black head to gray."

Hear how old John turns his quavers. What damned dull
music an Indian song is, after all, Major! I wonder if they ever
sing by note (p. 162).

Chingachgook is also drunk and singing, but it is "a kind of wild,
melancholy air . . . only understood by himself and Natty" (p.
162). No one is paying any attention to him; some of the
townsmen are discussing "the treatment of mangy hogs" or Mr.
Grant's sermon, while the village doctor is explaining Oliver's
gunshot wound to Judge Temple. Chingachgook's face, in the
meantime, has assumed "an expression very much like brutal
ferocity" (p. 163). Finally, his song interrupts the other conversa-
tions, and Natty is chosen by Cooper to quiet the Indian down.
This he does, but only after he has rebuked Chingachgook for
singing about past battles, "when the worst enemy of all is near
you, and keeps the Young Eagle from his rights." "I have fought
in as many battles as any warrior in your tribe," Natty says, "but
cannot boast of my deeds at such a time as this." It is Oliver "who
should speak aloud, where his voice is now too low to be heard"
(p. 163). Oliver, of course, does not speak until his grandfather
is discovered, and his silence, aside from furthering the mystery
of Cooper's plot, is another example of the victimization of those
characters in *The Pioneers* who are unable to resist (except in
occasional passionate speeches) the "civilizing" of the wilderness.
It is not surprising, therefore, that the villagers' only response to
Chingachgook's wild resentment in the Bold Dragoon is a brief,
almost symbolic gesture of self-assurance and scorn from
Richard Jones:

> The appeal of the hunter seemed in some measure to recall
> the confused faculties of the Indian, who turned his face to-
> wards the listeners and gazed intently on the Judge. . . . His
> hand seemed to make a fruitless effort to release his to-
> mahawk which was confined by its handle to his belt, while his
> eyes gradually became vacant. Richard at that instant thrust-
> ing a mug before him, his features changed to the grin of
> idiocy, and seizing the vessel with both hands, he sank back-
> ward on the bench and drank until satiated, when he made an

effort to lay aside the mug with the helplessness of total inebri-
ety (p. 164).

Nowhere in all of Cooper's novels is there a scene that surpas-
ses the real pathos of this one. Somehow the drunken Indian's
fruitless effort to raise his tomahawk and Squire Jones's smug
reliance on the "white man's tomahawk" to pacify the Indian
come closer to the imaginative truth of *The Pioneers* than any
other single episode in the novel. In its totality of vision, it cap-
tures both the injustice and the inevitability of social change.

But again, it is one thing for Cooper to depict the Indians
and Natty as the victims of social change and the amoral forces
of history, and another thing to conclude, in a spirit that is
quite out of character for Natty, that "the time will come when
right will be done; and we must have patience" (p. 164).
Whether Natty is referring to this life or the next, this advice is
still Cooper's way of evaluating Christianity (and its patron, social progress) according to its principles, rather than its practice.
By failing to call a spade a spade, Cooper retreats into a
philosophy of resignation that is closer to Chingachgook's passiv-
ity than to Natty's customary bitterness. Violence, from this
standpoint, is a worse sin than injustice. No matter how much
Cooper would have liked to distribute his sympathies (and the
sympathies of his readers) in *The Pioneers* between the victors
and victims of history, it could not be done convincingly.

The questions raised by Cooper are never finally answered;
but they are questions that are largely evaded in his other novels.
Must the injustices of history be recognized and condemned,
even though true justice may have to wait until the Last Judge-
ment? If so, to what extent can and should the individual condemn the forces of social change, without losing himself in his
nostalgic memories of better times? At what point, in other
words, does the act of moral judgment or its absence (on the part
of a character or his author) become self-deceptive and ironic?
Cooper is divided against himself on the answers to these questions: Chingachgook embodies a pathetic loss of identity (except

in memory) that Cooper, nevertheless, seemed to admire in its "Christian" manifestations; Judge Temple is driven to abrogate his judgment of history by a vision of a stable social order in the future; and Natty, whose bitterness toward the "civilizing" of Nature is, imaginatively, the most convincing and dignified response to history in *The Pioneers*, is saved from the ultimate act of resignation by the wilderness that still stretches to the west of him. "I have took but little comfort," Natty tells Elizabeth, "sin' your father come on with his settlers. . . . I know you mean all for the best, but our ways does n't agree: I love the woods, and ye relish the face of man. . . . The meanest of God's creatur's be made for some use, and I'm formed for the wilderness" (pp. 474, 475). Natty does not have to remain in society (although, ironically, he can never escape its advance guard in himself); "the habits of forty years" need not be "dispossessed by the ties of a day" (p. 475). Nor does Natty have to retain his bitterness and anger, once Major Effingham and Chingachgook have died. Cooper, in effect, can remain non committal about the final beneficence or harm of human history because his hero can escape its spiritual consequences.

Not so the heroes and heroines who are at odds with social change in later American novels: there is no alternative environment—social or natural—in which they can find a greater degree of stability and order. Unlike Natty, who can continually move away from the clearings, they are thrown back on their real or imagined visions of the past, in which they often hope to find a kind of moral immunity from and transcendence of history. When this happens, from Henry Adams's *Democracy* to A. B. Guthrie, Jr.'s *These Thousand Hills,* the author's conscious use of irony comes into play, and his answers to the questions mentioned above become far more conclusive than Cooper's. There may be dignity in resistance to social change and a touching pathos in the nostalgia for a stable social order; but there is only self-deception in assuming that such an order could ever be perpetuated (or even properly established) in a democratic society.

2

"The fluctuating waves of our social life": Nathaniel Hawthorne's *The House of the Seven Gables*

The justification for including Nathaniel Hawthorne's *The House of the Seven Gables* in a discussion of social change in American literature might seem tenuous, since the moral of the novel would appear to imply the opposite of change. Hawthorne's attempt "to connect a bygone time with the very present that is flitting away from us," as he says himself in his Preface, was based on "the truth, namely, that the wrong-doing of one generation lives into the successive ones."[1] And indeed, virtually every twist and turn of Hawthorne's plot is designed to show the same moral problem recurring in one generation after another. The "hard, stern, relentless look" on Judge Pyncheon's face, as well as the hardness of heart that it signifies, is an inheritance from the original Colonel Pyncheon of colonial Massachusetts—"a precious heirloom, from that bearded ancestor, in whose picture both the expression, and, to a singular degree, the features of the modern Judge were shown as by a kind of prophesy" (p. 314). And Hepzibah Pyncheon reaffirms the connection when she says to the Judge, "Alas, Cousin Jaffrey, this hard and grasping spirit has run in our blood these two

43

hundred years. You are but doing over again, in another shape, what your ancestor before you did, and sending down to your posterity the curse inherited from him!" (p. 386).

Very simply, in Hawthorne's view of history,

> the weaknesses and defects, the bad passions the mean tendencies, and the moral diseases which lead to crime are handed down from one generation to another, by a far surer process of transmission than human law has been able to establish in respect to the riches and honors which it seeks to entail upon posterity (p. 314).

And because *The House of the Seven Gables* was intended to be a "history of retribution for the sin of long ago" (p. 267)—namely, the original Colonel's persecution of Matthew Maule and the usurpation of his property—the greedy Judge's death must be caused by the same apoplectic seizure that killed his unscrupulous forebear. To complete Hawthorne's allegory, however, there must also be a Maule present—in the person of Holgrave, the young daguerrotypist, who reveals the Judge's sins and Clifford Pyncheon's innocence and then reclaims the Pyncheon property for his family by marrying Phoebe Pyncheon, a second cousin of the dead Judge. Though Phoebe retains the "family tone," her final marriage to the plebian Holgrave is meant to insure the extinction of all the bad blood in the Pyncheon family, whose race over the years, like the chickens at the old house, had "degenerated . . . in consequence of too strict a watchfulness to keep it pure" (p. 296).

This, in brief, is the apparent structure of continuity between past and present in *The House of the Seven Gables*. From father to son, Hawthorne says, the Pyncheons had "clung to [their] ancestral house with singular tenacity of home attachment" (p. 254). Legally, they were the rightful proprietors,

> but old Matthew Maule, it is to be feared, trode downward from his own age to a far later one, planting a heavy footstep, all the way, on the conscience of a Pyncheon. If so, we are left to dispose of the awful query, whether each inheritor of the property—conscious of wrong, and failing to rectify it—did

not commit anew the great guilt of his ancestor, and incur all its original responsibilities. And supposing such to be the case, would it not be a far truer mode of expression to say of the Pyncheon family, that they inherited a great misfortune, than the reverse? (p. 254).

Thus, the House of the Seven Gables is meant to be a special kind of spiritual or psychological property: it embodies "the folly of tumbling down an avalanche of ill-gotten gold, or real estate, on the heads of an unfortunate posterity, thereby to maim and crush them, until the accumulated mass shall be scattered abroad in its original atoms" (p. 243). And at the end of the novel, the remaining Pyncheons are, in fact, "scattered abroad" when Holgrave and Phoebe move from the old house, with Hepzibah and Clifford, to Judge Pyncheon's country estate, where they can begin again, like Chanticleer and his hens, "with an evident design, as a matter of duty and conscience, to continue their illustrious breed under better auspices than for a century past" (p. 433).

In short, Hawthorne attempted to adapt his hereditary drama of good and evil to the structure of history (a two-hundred-year period in this case, as opposed to the limited time span in his other novels). This technique, however, would have been more convincing if Hawthorne had permitted the conscience that he attributes to Judge Pyncheon to express itself at all. Then, perhaps, the House of the Seven Gables, as a reminder of the family sins, might have become the Judge's "great misfortune" and a convincing form of retribution in itself. But the Judge's guilt is never seen, nor are any other workings of his mind for that matter; Hawthorne only *mentions* that they exist. Consequently, the novel's process of moral retribution must operate *outside* the conscience of the individual, in the realm of dire prophesies, family curses, and hereditary diseases. The only character who is burdened with guilt feelings is Clifford Pyncheon, and these are neither directly related to the "bygone time" that Hawthorne was "connecting" with the present nor offered as the basic cause of Clifford's psychological confusion.

What is relatively absent from *The House of the Seven Gables* is Hawthorne's inspired feeling for what Henry James called the "latent romance of New England"—that element which he found in "the secret play of the Puritan faith." While Hawthorne's imagination, characteristically, could make little of the "common tasks and small conditions" of life in the democratic society about him, according to James, it "grew alert and irrepressible as it manoeuvered for the back view and turned up the under side of common aspects—the laws secretly broken, the impulses secretly felt, the hidden passions, the double lives, the dark corners, the closed rooms, the skeletons in the cupboard and at the feast."[2] Of all this, *The House of the Seven Gables* has far less than Hawthorne's other novels, and where it is present it is either unrelated to the Puritan faith per se (as in Clifford's impulse to jump from the window into the street) or it is a structural device to further the plot (as in Holgrave's "double life" as a Maule incognito). One could argue, in fact, that Hawthorne's imagination succeeds in *The House of the Seven Gables* in precisely that with which it was not concerned in his other novels: the presentation of the "common tasks and small conditions" of life. The major revelation of the novel, from this point of view, is a historical continuity, not a moral or spiritual continuity expressed in the form of allegory. In the context of the story, Hawthorne's general idea that all men are divided against themselves by conscience and guilt is presented much less effectively than his narrower, more specific perception that "in this republican country, amid the fluctuating waves of our social life, somebody is always at the drowning-point" (p. 265).

No doubt Hawthorne wanted all his novels to be considered romances in the sense that James used the term in the passage quoted above. In each he attempted to avoid the task of being faithful, "not merely to the possible, but to the probable and ordinary course of man's experience," as he says in his Preface to *The House of the Seven Gables* (p. 243). Instead, he looked for a historical connection that would, at the same time, be the kind of "poetic or fairy precinct" that he later found in Italy (p. 590).

And, in both *The Scarlet Letter* and *The Blithedale Romance*, Hawthorne did manage to find a distinct historical locale that, for his readers in the 1850s, was yet "a little removed from the highway of ordinary travel" (p. 439). The result, in each of these novels, was a setting that had its own inherent "romance" rising out of a passion for social perfection. If one thinks for a moment of the demanding ideals that characterize Hawthorne's Salem and Blithedale, as different as the two societies may be in the *content* of their faiths, one can easily see how Hawthorne was blessed, in each case, with a situation in which the very structure of each society was geared to the possible rather than the probable course of man's experience. In both environments, the standards for human conduct left a great deal of room for failure and for the kind of "spiritual contortions" that, in James's view, inspired Hawthorne's imagination. His characters, in effect, are just as concerned with the spiritual drama of their lives as was their author.

The situation is quite different in *The House of the Seven Gables*. There is much that is psychological, but little that is spiritual about the dilemma of Clifford and Hepzibah Pyncheon. Essentially, that dilemma is an inability to cope with the new in the form of a changing society, rather than an inability to cope with the old in the form of hereditary guilt. The first, as Hawthorne presents it, is a historical predicament, the second is an allegorical predicament. But Hawthorne never succeeds in combining the two convincingly. Both *The House of the Seven Gables* and Cooper's *The Pioneers* (compared to the later Leatherstocking tales) fail as romances and succeed as realistic novels for the same reason: namely, the persistent incompatibility, despite the authors' overt intentions, of history and morality.

Some important continuities between past and present still remain in *The House of the Seven Gables;* there is, as Hawthorne says in his opening paragraphs,

a connection with the long past—a reference to forgotten events and personages, and to manners, feelings, and opin-

ions, almost or wholly obsolete—which, if adequately translated to the reader, would serve to illustrate how much of old
material goes to make up the freshest novelty of human life (p.
245).

As simply a statement about the tenure of past habits of thought
and action, though out-of-date in the present, this seems to be an
excellent guide to the imaginative success of *The House of the
Seven Gables*. The obsolete manners, feelings, and opinions of
Clifford and Hepzibah Pyncheon represent a continuity that, at
the same time, highlights the discontinuity between itself and the
actual world outside the House of the Seven Gables. And nowhere is this more evident than in the chapters that come after
Hawthorne has recounted the story of the ancestral Pyncheons
and Maules and has begun "the real action of our tale."
Hepzibah's halting ordeal with her cent-shop in chapters two
through four establishes the tone of compassion and irony with
which Hawthorne describes the pathetic attempts of Clifford
and Hepzibah to take "a due part in the bustling world"
throughout the novel.[3] That ordeal is finally more compelling
than any story of crime and punishment that Hawthorne presents in *The House of the Seven Gables*.

Specifically in the early chapters of the novel, Hawthorne succeeds in showing how characteristic Hepzibah's predicament is
in a democracy, though to herself it may have seemed extraordinary and unbearable. Her illusions of self-importance are
comic to be sure, but they are no less real and sympathetic for
that reason. When she clumsily spills a tumbler of marbles in her
shop, for example, and stoops to pick them up, Hawthorne invokes the reader's understanding as well as his sense of humor:

> As her rigid and rusty frame goes down upon its hand and
> knees, in quest of the absconding marbles, we positively feel so
> much the more inclined to shed tears of sympathy, from the
> very fact that we must needs turn aside and laugh at her. For
> here, —and if we fail to impress it suitably upon the reader, it
> is our own fault, not that of the theme,—*here is one of the truest
> points of melancholy interest that occur in ordinary life*. It was the
> final throe of what called itself old gentility. A lady—who had

fed herself from childhood with the shadowy food of aristocratic reminiscences, and whose religion it was that a lady's
hand soils itself irremediably by doing aught for bread—this
born lady, after sixty years of narrowing means, is fain to step
down from her pedestal of imaginary rank. . . . The tragedy is
enacted with as continual a repetition as that of a popular
drama on a holiday; and, nevertheless, is felt as deeply,
perhaps, as when an hereditary noble sinks below his order.
More deeply; since, with us, rank is the grosser substance of
wealth and a splendid establishment, and has no spiritual existence after the death of these, but dies hopelessly along with
them (p. 265; italics added).

In its ordinariness and its finality, Hepzibah's situation is both
ironic and pathetic. On the one hand, she is justly terrified at the
idea of "coming into sordid contact with the world, from which
she had so long kept aloof" (p. 266); yet, on the other hand,
there is nothing at all singular about her fate. "In the town of her
nativity," Hawthorne says, "we might point to several little shops
of a similar description, some of them in houses as ancient as
that of the Seven Gables; and one or two, it may be, where a
decayed gentlewoman stands behind the counter, as grim an
image of family pride as Miss Hepzibah Pyncheon herself" (p.
266).

In the end, the reader does not need the sensational aspects of
the Pyncheon history to account for this family pride in Hepzibah, and Hawthorne himself seems to have sensed this discrepancy:

How can we elevate our history of retribution for the sin of
long ago, when, as one of our most prominent figures, we are
compelled to introduce—not a young and lovely woman, nor
even the stately remains of beauty, storm-shattered by
affliction—but a gaunt, sallow, rusty-jointed maiden, in a
long-waisted silk gown, and with the strange horror of a tur-
ban on her head! . . . Her great life-trial seems to be, that,
after sixty years of idleness, she finds it convenient to earn
comfortable bread by setting up a shop in a small way.
Nevertheless, if we look through all the heroic fortunes of
mankind, we shall find this same entanglement of something

mean and trivial with whatever is noblest in joy or sorrow. Life is made up of marble and mud. And, without all the deeper trust in a comprehensive sympathy above us, we might hence be led to suspect the insult of a sneer, as well as an immitigable frown, on the iron countenance of fate. What is called poetic insight is the gift of discerning, in this sphere of strangely mingled elements, the beauty and the majesty which are compelled to assume a garb so sordid (p. 267).

Hawthorne is here finding his poetry in the probable rather than the possible circumstances of life; and the appearance, at the end of the novel, of "a comprehensive sympathy above us" in the form of a deus ex machina that saves Hepzibah and her brother from economic hardship, does not alter the reader's vision of a "sneer" on "the iron countenance of fate"—or, in this case, on the iron countenance of history. There is no real romance or retribution in the ordinary fluctuations of society, at least not in *The House of the Seven Gables*.

The character of Holgrave is there, in one sense, to make this point clear. In chapter 3, it is he who brings out, rather mercilessly, the ironies of Hepzibah's situation. When he enters her shop, she cries on his shoulder that she "never can go through with it. . . . The world is too chill and hard,—and I am too old, and too feeble, and too hopeless! . . . I am a woman," she insists, piteously, "I was going to say, a lady,—but I consider that as past" (p. 269). To this Holgrave replies, with "a strange gleam of half-hidden sarcasm flashing through the kindliness of his manner," that

no matter if it be past! Let it go! . . . Hitherto, the lifeblood has been gradually chilling in your veins as you sat aloof, within your circle of gentility, while the rest of the world was fighting out its battle with one kind of necessity or another. . . . These names of gentleman and lady had a meaning, in the past history of the world, and conferred privileges, desirable or otherwise, on those entitled to bear them. In the present—and still more in the future condition of society—they imply, not privilege, but restriction! (p. 269).

Holgrave is too optimistic perhaps about Hepzibah's ability to overcome her fears and join the "united struggle of mankind"; but he is certainly right about the uselessness of her habits of thought in a changing society and their power to imprison her in the past. The more she encounters "the temper and manners of what she termed the lower classes," the more she envisions herself "occupying a sphere of unquestionable superiority" (p. 275). And, thus, during her first day of business, the "aristocratic" Hepzibah begins "to fear that the shop would prove her ruin in a moral and religious point of view, without contributing very essentially towards even her temporal welfare" (p. 276). It is fear like this, as well as Hepzibah's cherished hope "that some harlequin trick of fortune would intervene in her favor" (p. 281), that Holgrave frequently exposes as nostalgic and illusory. Yet, at the end of the novel, Holgrave himself becomes the key figure in a "harlequin trick of fortune" that does save Hepzibah from poverty and returns to her the dignity of wealth and status.

The problem with the character of Holgrave, throughout the novel, is that he must perform two roles: one in service to Hawthorne's historical vision of social change and the anxieties it creates for time-stricken characters like Clifford and Hepzibah, and the other in service to Hawthorne's allegorical preoccupation with the hereditary drama of good and evil. Henry James described Holgrave's first role as "a kind of national type—that of the young citizen of the United States whose fortune is simply is his lively intelligence, and who stands naked, as it were, unbiased and unemcumbered alike, in the center of the far-stretching level of American life." While there is some question whether Holgrave, in this sense, is as "unbiased" as James said, his character does function "as a contrast": "his lack of traditions, his democratic stamp, his condensed experience, are opposed to the dessicated prejudices and exhausted vitality of the race of which poor feebly-scowling, rusty-jointed Hepzibah is the most heroic representative."[4] By the end of the novel, however, Holgrave's fortune (in every sense of the word) is no longer simply the result of his "lively intelligence," but rather of his "biased" and "encumbered" lineage. Before he met Phoebe, he had had a varied, adventurous career and, "amid all these personal vicissitudes, . . . had never lost his identity"; though not very affectionate, "he had never violated the innermost man, but had carried his conscience along with him" (p. 349). As such, Phoebe had no particular interest in him. Only after Holgrave's lively intelligence is sacrificed for a tolerable conservatism ("a happy man," he finally decides, "inevitably confines himself within ancient limits" [p. 428]) and his identity as a representative of the "old wizard," Matthew Maule, is made public, can the novel come to a close with his marriage to Phoebe.

The difficulty here is not that Hawthorne saw an irony in Holgrave's historical position; indeed, Holgrave's faith in social change, in "a golden era, to be accomplished in his own lifetime," will never fully be satisfied. He simply shares the necessary, but naive, hope "of every century since the epoch of Adam's grandchildren—that in this age, more than ever before, the moss-grown and rotten Past is to be torn down, and lifeless institutions to be thrust out of the way, and their dead corpses buried, and everything to begin anew" (p. 350). Throughout *The House of the Seven Gables,* Hawthorne reserves his most successful ironies for those characters who see history—either in the form of tradition or in the form of social change—as a force that justifies their status or desires. Thus, the Pyncheon aristocracy, with its "mysterious and terrible past" embodied in the old house, will decay in time for the same reason that Holgrave's illusions about the "golden era" must finally be modified by experience. Eventually, as Hawthorne says, Holgrave will probably become another one of those "young men" in America

for whom we anticipate wonderful things, but of whom, even after much and careful inquiry, we never happen to hear another word. The effervescence of youth and passion, and the fresh gloss of the intellect and imagination, endow them with a false brilliancy, which makes fools of themselves and other people. Like certain chintzes, calicoes, and ginghams, they show finely in their first newness, but cannot stand the sun and rain, and assume a very sober aspect after washingday (pp. 351–52).

All this is consistent with Hawthorne's vision of American history as a "common and inevitable movement onward" (p. 397). But Hawthorne, in the end, could not permit Holgrave's faith to take its own course to probable compromise. Instead of allowing his identity as a historical type to remain intact, Hawthorne substituted a new, unintended irony for the old, by compromising his character's integrity before its time. When Hawthorne has Holgrave mellow at the end of the novel, it is not merely because the youthful adventurer, in time, must barter "the haughty faith, with which he began life" for "a far humbler one at its close," but because Hawthorne had to divest Holgrave of his identity as a "representative of many compeers in his native land" (p. 351) in order for him to fulfill his function as the recipient, through marriage, of all the wealth and security previously possessed by the family that had persecuted his ancestors. For all his hatred of "dead men's houses," Holgrave must eventually settle with Phoebe in Judge Pyncheon's country estate, so that the descendants of Matthew Maule can complete Hawthorne's "history of retribution." By doing so, however, Holgrave becomes a premature advocate of "permanence," and history threatens to repeat itself, as it does when Natty Bumppo moves west.

Thus, Holgrave's historical identity as a "national type" and his allegorical identity as a Maule prove in the end somewhat contradictory. Everything he says and does in the novel can, in retrospect, be interpreted as the action of a Maule in search of justice and truth; but if this is the case, then his "unencumbered" spirit is surely suspect. He simply can not successfully bear the weight of two roles.

Hawthorne was aware of this predicament and tried to use Phoebe Pyncheon to modify Holgrave's historical identity before the novel's conclusion. When Holgrave cries, "What slaves we are to bygone times . . . we live in dead men's houses," she confidently replies, "why not, so long as we can be comfortable in them?" (pp. 352, 353). And eventually, Holgrave is swayed by his temptress as Adam was by his; like Eve, Phoebe is infinitely ingratiating and adaptable. Somehow, because of her combination of aristocratic and democratic blood (her father having married beneath his rank), she is less set in her ways than the other characters in *The House of the Seven Gables* and can there-

fore mediate between the extremes of historical types represented by Holgrave and the Pyncheons. She is identified with
no particular society, though "out of New England," Hawthorne
says, "it would be impossible to meet with a person combining so
many lady-like attributes with so many others that form no
necessary (if compatible) part of the character" (p. 291). While
Holgrave is distinguished by "his culture and his want of culture," Phoebe "shocked no canon of taste" and "never jarred
against surrounding circumstances" (pp. 351, 291). She has perfect manners, and yet no manners to identify her. In short,
Hawthorne must apologize for her "unreal" character:

> Instead of discussing her claim to rank among ladies, it would
> be preferable to regard Phoebe as the example of feminine
> grace and availability combined, in a state of society, if there
> were any such, where ladies did not exist. There it should be
> woman's office to move in the midst of practical affairs, and to
> gild them all, the very homeliest,—were it even the scouring
> of pots and kettles,—with an atmosphere of loveliness and joy
> (p. 291).

In this respect, Hawthorne contends that Phoebe stands for
"new Plebianism" as opposed to Hepzibah's "old Gentility"; but
the parallel is unconvincing. Hepzibah at least has a social context that supports her own "lady-like" existence, however narrow and obsolete it may be. For Phoebe, on the other hand, one
can only *imagine* a state of society, as Hawthorne admits, that will
give her character credibility. To the reader, as well as to Clifford Pyncheon, she seems a "symbol," rather than an "actual
fact."

If Phoebe has an infinitely adaptable character, Clifford and
Hepzibah are her antitheses. More than any other previous
figures in American literature, they do "jar" against surrounding
circumstances. The "shrinkage and extinction," as James put it,
of their aristocratic heritage[5] is best reflected in their own inability to cope with the changing society around them. Clifford's
confusion, for example, over the modern vehicles of transportation (cabs, omnibuses, and railroad) that he can see from his

window in the old house prompts Hawthorne's reflection that "nothing gives a sadder sense of decay than this loss or suspension of the power to deal with unaccustomed things, and to keep up with the swiftness of the passing moment" (p. 339). As the last vestiges of a more stable, pre-Revolutionary society, Clifford and his sister represent those victims of democracy who were, in de Tocqueville's words, "at the top of the late gradations of rank [and] cannot immediately forget their former greatness; they will long regard themselves as aliens in the midst of the newly composed society."[6]

Yet, while they are confused and frightened by the present, they also hate the past that entraps them. When Hepzibah makes her first sale in the little shop, she feels that "the structure of ancient aristocracy had been demolished" by "the sordid stain of that copper coin," but a moment later the experience gives her "a thrill of almost youthful enjoyment." "It was the invigorating breath," Hawthorne says, "of a fresh outward atmosphere, after the long torpor and monotonous seclusion of her life" (p. 273). If she is disgusted by the lower-class manners of her customers, she must also, at the same time, "struggle against a bitter emotion of a directly opposite kind: a sentiment of virulence, we mean, toward the idle aristocracy to which it had so recently been her pride to belong" (p. 275). Likewise, Clifford is at once drawn to and repelled by both the past and the present. Balancing above the procession of life in the streets of the town, he feels "a shivering repugnance at the idea of personal contact with the world," yet he is barely restrained from "plunging into the surging stream of human sympathies"—the "mighty river of life, massive in its tide, and black with mystery, and, out of its depths, calling to the kindred depth within him" (pp. 341, 342). To merge with that tide, with the process of social change that has swept past Clifford and Hepzibah during the decades of their physical and psychological isolation, is impossible, except through an act of self-destruction. Whether they resort, like Hepzibah, to "the shadowy food of aristocratic reminiscences" or, like Clifford, to the longing for a second childhood, they are still imprisoned by past habits of thought.

The mental state in which they are trapped is referred to by Hawthorne either as "one's own heart" or as the House of the Seven Gables itself. In fact, Hawthorne repeatedly uses the latter, in a larger sense, as an image of Clifford's mind, in much the same way that Poe used Roderick Usher's mansion as an image of its owner's mind. The old house is initially described as "a great human heart, with a life of its own, and full of rich and sombre reminiscences" (p. 258). Conversely, Clifford's struggling spirit, thanks to Phoebe's effervescence, is "doing its best to kindle the heart's household fire, and light up intellectual lamps in the dark and ruinous mansion, where it was doomed to be a forlorn inhabitant" (p. 306). The point that Hawthorne is so skillfully emphasizing with these interchangeable images is this: the darkest and most inexorable jailor is indeed one's own heart, particularly if, in a republican country, one has become isolated in and identified with a static representation of past prestige.

As the larger society around them has changed, Clifford's and Hepzibah's manners have become inflexible. The greater the discontinuity between past and present, in other words, the greater is their anxiety and their longing for a respite from change. The impulse to merge with the present, though unavailing, is almost as strong in them as their fear of the present. But their impulse, in the end, is exactly that—an impulse—while their fear is a habit. Consequently, some of the most dramatic moments in the novel are the result of their failure to realize how confined they are by their accustomed world.

Chapter 17, "The Flight of Two Owls," is the most conspicuous example. Hepzibah and Clifford are "like children in their experience" as they leave the old house after Cousin Jaffrey's death; isolated from a changing society for much of their lives, their feelings are a combination of fear and desperate resolution. Though in Hepzibah's mind "there was the wretched consciousness of being adrift" in "the world's broad, bleak atmosphere," she allows herself to be guided by the "powerful excitement" that possesses Clifford (p. 395). At no time does Hawthorne let the reader escape the feeling that their hopes of beginning life anew are an illusion. Whether the atmosphere of the world into which they are entering is actually "comfortless" is unimportant; that is the way it must appear to those who have so long remained "above the surface of society" (p. 289). For Hepzibah, and eventually for Clifford, the sense of change is too sudden and incomprehensible: "any certainty," she thinks, "would have been preferable to this" (p. 396).

Significantly, Hawthorne does not merely have them depart from house and town by an arbitrary means of transportation: they must choose the fastest escape possible, the vehicle that is most characteristic of the new society that threatens their past "certainties." Thus, the railroad, in Hawthorne's hands, becomes a metaphor that at once attracts and overpowers the wanderers:

> At last, therefore, and after so long estrangement from everything that the world acted or enjoyed, they had been drawn into the great current of human life, and were swept away with it, as by the suction of fate itself (p. 397).

Psychologically as well as visually, "everything was unfixed from its age-long rest, and moving at whirlwind speed in a direction opposite to their own" (p. 397). Though to Hepzibah the train ride seems like a dream and to Clifford, reality, in truth it is neither and both. It is a reality that, by its dreamlike nature, challenges and exposes their own dreams of society. What is significant for them is the *relative* difference between the physical and psychological permanence of their life in the old house and the physical and psychological impermanence of their experience on the train.

In addition to the speed of the train, the two travelers are also confused by the society it transports. No one seems upset or inconvenienced: everyone else is used to the "rapid current of affairs," so unlike the Pyncheon style of life. And because the train is filled with those persons who are able to accept the changing environment it represents, the journey for them is "life itself"—"the common and inevitable movement onward." Clifford sees this, but deceives himself into thinking that he and Hepzibah can become a part of all they survey: "You are thinking of that dismal old house, and of Cousin Jaffrey," he tells Hepzibah reproachfully. "Take my advice,—follow my example,—and let such things slip aside. Here we are, in the world, Hepzibah!—in the midst of life!—in the throng of our fellow beings! Let you and I be happy!" (p. 398). But Hepzibah can neither see the value of Clifford's advice, nor share his confidence in their ability to be happy in the midst of life. She can not escape her mental image of the old house:

> With miles and miles of varied scenery between, there was no scene for her, save the seven old gable-peaks. . . . This one old house was everywhere! It transported its great, lumbering bulk with more than railroad speed, and set itself phlegmatically down on whatever spot she glanced at (p. 398).

As if he were reading Hepzibah's mind, Clifford proceeds to mock man's willingness to permit his physical environment to confine his spirit; the railroad is the benefactor of man because it will force him to move and change:

> Why should he make himself a prisoner for life in brick, and stone, and old worm-eaten timber, when he may just as easily dwell, in one sense, nowhere,—in a better sense, wherever the fit and beautiful shall offer him a home? . . . The greatest possible stumbling-blocks in the path of human happiness and improvement are these heaps of bricks and stones, consolidated with mortar, or hewn timber, fastened together with spike-nails, which men painfully contrive for their own torment, and call them house and home! (pp. 399, 400).

Clifford is right, of course, except for the fact that he fails to see himself as a "prisoner for life"—a condition that neither the destruction of the House of the Seven Gables nor the death of Judge Pyncheon can alleviate. It is too late for Hepzibah and Clifford; their physical environment has become their mental environment, and escaping from the old house will not change anything. The point is made when Clifford realizes that the electric telegraph—another wonder of the new age—will pursue a criminal (as he thinks of himself) faster than he can flee his accustomed environment. His world again becomes all-confining, his hopes depart, and he and Hepzibah leave the train at a lonely way-station. She then must be his guide and can only pray, "Have mercy on us!," to the God whom Hawthorne earlier called "the sole worker of realities" (pp. 403, 351).

But, by rights, there should be no mercy for the two "ghosts," at least not the kind of freedom that Clifford envisioned on the train. After they return to the old house, Holgrave helps to relieve Clifford's fears, reveal the Pyncheon sins, and restore the identity and rights of the Maules. Clifford can never be fully cleared of any complicity in Jaffrey's death: "no great mistake, whether acted or endured, in our mortal sphere, is ever really set right. Time, the continual viscissitude of circumstances, and the invariable inopportunity of death, render it impossible" (p. 432). So Clifford must live with that stigma; yet Hawthorne continues to shelter him from the greater, social consequences of the Pyncheon heritage. The author, in effect, becomes the God to which Hepzibah prayed—and mercifully allows Clifford to reexperience some of his lost youth. Holgrave takes Clifford and Hepzibah away to Judge Pyncheon's country estate (one of those "stumbling-blocks in the path of human happiness and improvement"), away from the threat of a changing world, and there Clifford is permitted to enjoy a measure of "the fit and beautiful" that he imagined on the train. Though, as Hawthorne generiously concedes, Clifford

> never, it is true, attained to nearly the full measure of what might have been his faculties, . . . he was evidently happy. Could we pause to give another picture of his daily life, with all the appliances now at command to gratify his instinct for the Beautiful, the garden scenes, that seemed so sweet to him, would look mean and trivial in comparison (p. 432).

The House of the Seven Gables, like *The Pioneers,* manifests a frustrating combination of a genial and pious wish, on the one hand, and a stern historical vision, on the other. Perhaps this is because both Hawthorne and Cooper had themselves experienced what Phoebe Pyncheon refers to as the "dizzying" effect of "a shifting world" (p. 353); hence their desire to exempt a Natty Bumppo or a Clifford Pyncheon from the final rigors and total disillusionment of historical change. In Hawthorne as in Cooper, the idea of history remains, by and large, a moral idea—a question of right and wrong as well as of change and necessity. But in the eight novels discussed in the following chapters, the recognition of social change as an irrevocable fact of life is less qualified. The past that is going or gone can not be retrieved in one's memory or imagination without one's becoming enmeshed in self-deception; thus, the authors of these novels maintain to a greater extent than Cooper or Hawthorne a consistent, ironic detachment that allows them to accept the consequences of history. Unlike Cooper and Hawthorne, who could not relinquish the idea of historical retribution in *The Pioneers* and *The House of the Seven Gables,* these authors based their stories on the raw, unromantic workings of history.

3
Visiting the "engine-room": Henry Adams's *Democracy*

It is to be regretted that the best American political novel should have received so little critical attention since its publication in 1880, a situation due in part to the fact that its author was primarily a historian and wrote only one other novel (*Esther*). But Henry Adams's *Democracy* has also suffered the literary fate of nearly every novel of its kind: either it has been interpreted as history—Senator Ratcliffe, in reality, was James G. Blaine, the President was Rutherford B. Hayes, and so forth; or it has been approached as a statement of political philosophy—no more, no less a work of fiction that *The Education.* "The danger was, and still is," as Henry David Aiken has recently observed, "That its readers would regard the novel as merely a clever satire, verging at times uncomfortably close to burlesque, of a particular episode in the history of American democracy. Viewed simply as a political fable, it is more than that."[1] Indeed it is. To read Adam's novel as only a clever satire or an autobiographical document is to miss, in general, the complexity of its characters and their interrelationships and, in particular, its subtlest ironies.

This is a distinct possibility for the reader who casually equates the author of *Democracy* with its apparent heroine. There was a side of Henry Adams that wanted not merely to touch the levers of political power, but, like Mrs. Lightfoot Lee, to judge the men and events of history according to the moral principles he would have used to guide his own conduct as a practical politician. However, there was another side of Henry Adams that was willing to acknowledge and live with the possibility that history—in all its twists and turns—had nothing whatever to do with morality. And this is where he and Mrs. Lee part company. She could not have accepted his conclusion in *The Education* that history was "in essence incoherent and immoral" and that, as such, "the times had long passed when a student could stop before chaos or order; he had no choice but to march with his world."[2] *Democracy* presents, dramatically, a similar vision of history characterized by social change. At times in the novel there is even the suggestion that the historical nature of things may always have been the same—but to Mrs. Lee, the central character, the changing society around her appears to be a new and original threat to the stability of the past.

To be sure, at the outset of the novel, Mrs. Lee displays a readiness to "march with her world."[3] She goes to Washington to feel the pulse of the nation, "to touch with her own hand the massive machinery of society; to measure with her own mind the capacity of the motive power" (p. 10). "Since her husband's death, five years before," Adams says, "she had lost her taste for New York society" (p. 1). After plunging into philosophy and then philanthropy, she was left with only the frustrated feeling that

all the paupers and criminals in New York might henceforward rise in their majesty and manage every railway on the continent. . . . She could find nothing in [New York] that seemed to demand salvation. What gave peculiar sanctity to numbers? Why were a million people, who all resembled each other, any way more interesting than one person? What aspiration could she help to put into the mind of this great million-armed monster that would make it worth her love or respect? (p. 3).

Was it ambition, Adams asks—the desire to find an "object worth a sacrifice"—or "mere restlessness" that prompted Mrs. Lee's bitterness toward "American life in general and all life in particular" (p. 4)? She did not want social position, thanks to her father, a respectable Philadelphia clergyman, and her late husband, a descendant of the Virginia Lees. As a widow, Mrs. Lee at least had enough money for the best clothes and furniture, as well as occasional trips to Europe. Yet, despite the wealth and the eminent respectability of her social position in New York, she could not escape the feeling that American society, in the larger sense, had somehow evaded her and was moving onward, without her understanding it in the least. "It was the feeling of a passenger on an ocean steamer whose mind will not give him rest until he has been in the engine-room and talked with the engineer" (p. 10).

But Mrs. Lee's shift in locale and atmosphere is by no means a rejection of her former society. In truth, she only seeks "what amusement there might be in politics"; and if her experience in Washington turned out to be as "dreary" as her friends predicted, then that would be sufficient for her (p. 11). What she ultimately desires is an exposure to a "swarm of ordinary people" that will dispel the ennui of her life in New York. She decides that if Washington society does justify the warnings of her friends, then "she should have gained all she wanted, for it would be a pleasure to return,—precisely," Adams adds, "the feeling she longed for" (p. 11). Thus, Mrs. Lee moves to Washington carrying the baggage of her past habits, which will, she hopes, be made bearable again, through a new knowledge of American history—the kind of knowledge that would give her a feeling of greater appreciation and control over the course of her own more exclusive society. "What she wanted," Adams says, "was POWER"—the moral power, specifically, that comes with a faith in one's social superiority.

Unfortunately, what she finds in Washington is not the reassuring spectacle she desired. The vortex of political and historical power that has its center there is neither comprehensible nor resistible. She soon discovers that, for men like Silas Ratcliffe, the powerful Senator from Illinois, history bears little, if any, resemblance to virtue; it is something that must be obeyed and, if possible, survived by whatever means necessary. Democracy, a Washington acquaintance tells Mrs. Lee at one point, is simply "the inevitable consequence of what has gone before it. . . . Every other possible step is backward, and I do not care to repeat the past. . . . Let us be true to our time, Mrs. Lee! If our age is to be beaten, let us die in the ranks" (pp. 77, 78). For society and politician alike, the primary rule is survival of the fittest, not survival of the most virtuous.

The unfolding of these ideas and personalities, in which Mrs. Lee vainly hopes, in the beginning, to be a spectator rather than a participant, begins with her December arrival in the Capital. When she enters her newly rented house, the "curious barbarism of the curtains and the wall-papers" prompts in her a "mingled expression of contempt and grief" (p. 13)—an initial indication of her inability, or unwillingness, to adapt to a new environment. By transforming "that benighted and heathen residence" into a "nobler conception of duty and existence" (p. 14), she reveals the "tacit assumption of superior refinement" that guides her thinking throughout the novel and, eventually, drives her back to her old way of life.

Here at the beginning of the novel, however, she has determinedly come to learn and, even more, to judge.

> She wanted to learn how the machinery of government worked, and what was the quality of men who controlled it. One by one, she passed them through her crucibles, and tested them by acids and by fire (p. 20).

One of her tests for impurities, designed to support her own sense of superiority, is flattery. This she uses with great success on Senator Ratcliffe at an early dinner party; her purpose is simply "to turn him inside out; to experiment on him and use him as young physiologists use frogs and kittens. If there was good or bad in him, she meant to find its meaning" (pp. 36–37). She has to know "whether America is right or wrong," pure or corrupt, and Senator Ratcliffe is the type who will determine her answer. "I really want to know whether to believe in Mr. Ratcliffe," she says. "If I throw him overboard, everything must go, for he is only a specimen" (p. 76). Yet the inconsistency of using deception and false impressions to discover if Ratcliffe is honest and forthright does not seem to bother Mrs. Lee.

What increasingly annoys her the closer she gets to the heart of American politics is her conviction that, from the first to the last President, it was all a "melancholy spectacle": "what vexations, what disappointments, what grievous mistakes, what very objectionable manners!" (p. 84). American politicians, whether mighty or lowly, apparently

> had no great problems of thought to settle, no questions that rose above the ordinary rules of common morals and homely duty. How they had managed to befog the subject! What elaborate show-structures they had built up, with no result but to obscure the horizon! (p. 84).

Even the great Senator Ratcliffe, by his own admission, "had very little sympathy for thin moralising, and a statesmanlike contempt for philosophical politics. He loved power, and he meant to be President. That was enough" (p. 85). Could the country really have done worse without men like him, Mrs. Lee wonders? "What deeper abyss could have opened under the nation's feet, than that to whose verge they brought it?" (p. 84).

This rhetorical pessimism might be just an expression of Henry Adams's own convictions if it were not for the fact that Mrs. Lee, because of her high expectations or, rather, her moral pretentiousness, is in many ways more mistaken and "objectionable" in her aristocratic manners than are the politicians she so rigorously examines. In all the crowd at the new President's first evening reception, there is no one besides Mrs. Lee who feels "the mockery of this exhibition," no one else who is shocked by the obvious resemblance of the President and his wife to stupid, mechanical "toy dolls." Mrs. Lee "groans in spirit" while everyone else seems to accept the whole affair as a "regular part of the President's duty" with "nothing ridiculous about it" (p. 87). Of course, she may be right about the fatuity of the reception, but she is very wrong in assuming that everyone takes the proceedings more seriously than she does. For them it is a necessary democratic formality; for her it is "worse than anything in the 'Inferno' " (p. 88). Much to Mrs. Lee's chagrin, the President and his wife are, in truth, "representatives of the society which streamed past them"—the central figures in "the slowly eddying dance of Democracy" (pp. 86, 88); thus, Mrs. Lee's criticism of the "droll aping of monarchial forms" at the Presidential reception is not essentially an antiaristocratic sentiment. It is the unanimity of participation rather than the "monarchial forms" themselves that offends her. She herself, the novel suggests, would have felt much more at home in a more aristocratic society where, in de Tocqueville's phrase, "men are astonishingly unlike each other" while, at the same time, every man remains "pretty stationary in his own sphere." It upsets Mrs. Lee to observe a democratic society in which everything changes yet "all men are alike and do things pretty nearly alike."[4]

Perhaps Mrs. Lee's disposition to regret a society that is, at once, changing and homogeneous is most obvious on the trip to Mount Vernon in chapter 6. The time is February, when the weather becomes summerlike and the political scene is notably in flux, reeking, Adams says, "with the thick atmosphere of bargain and sale. The old is going; the new is coming" (p. 114). The question at hand is the character and times of George Washington, raised by the flighty Victoria Dare in order to scandalize a visiting Irishman, Lord Dunbeg. According to Victoria, the "Father of his country" was "a raw-boned country farmer, very hard-featured, very awkward, very illiterate and very dull; very bad tempered, very profane, and generally tipsy after dinner" (pp. 123–24). Lord Dunbeg is duly shocked, and the others are amused. But the discussion does not end there. After Senator Ratcliffe has credited Washington with a "consciousness of inferior powers," a "dread of responsibility," and a desire to stand outside of politics with "sort of royal airs," John Carrington, a

Virginian lawyer, comes to Washington's defense. "Mr. Ratcliffe," he interposes sarcastically, "means that Washington was too respectable for our time" (p. 140). From this, Mrs. Lee seizes upon the idea that the first President may have been a rare paragon of virtue in a long line of corrupt politicians, to which Carrington cheerfully assents. Ratcliffe's final rebuttal is to dismiss entirely the relevance of Washington's character, even if it were virtuous:

> Public men . . . cannot be dressing themselves to-day in Washington's old clothes. If Washington were President now, he would have to learn our ways or lose the next election. Only fools and theorists imagine that our society can be handled with gloves or long poles. One must make one's self a part of it. If virtue won't answer our purpose, we must use vice, or our opponents will put us out of office, and this was as true in Washington's day as it is now, and always will be (p. 141).

Mrs. Lee, however, is unconvinced. As the boat leaves for the Capitol, she is still musing on the question, her imagination thoroughly captured by the legend of Washington's times:

> Was she, unknown to herself, gradually becoming tainted with the life about her? or was Ratcliffe right in accepting the good and the bad together, and in being of his time since he was in it? Why was it, she said bitterly to herself, that everything Washington touched, he purified, even down to the associations of his house? and why is it that everything we touch seems spoiled? Why do I feel unclean when I look at Mount Vernon? In spite of Mr. Ratcliffe, is it not better to be a child and to cry for the moon and stars? (p. 144).

Mrs. Lee's habit of moral intensity has already answered this last question: she would rather cling to her vision of an ethically pure historical period than accept the possibility that moral considerations may have no bearing on the course of history and that perhaps, as Ratcliffe says, "this was as true in Washington's day as it is now, and always will be."

In this moralistic approach to past and present society, John Carrington is Mrs. Lee's principal sympathizer throughout the novel. Essentially, theirs is an alliance of sorrow and memory that results, in part, from her pity for him as a member "of that unfortunate generation in the south which began existence with civil war . . . perhaps the more unfortunate because, like most educated Virginians of the old Washington school, he had seen from the first that, whatever issue the war took, Virginia and he must be ruined" (p. 21). Carrington, Adams continues quite compassionately, "had something of the dignity—others call it stiffness—of the old Virginia school, and twenty years of constant responsibility [for his mother and sisters on their worn-out plantation] and deferred hope had added a touch of care that bordered closely on sadness" (p. 22). From Mrs. Lee's point of view, Carrington is a heroic type—"my idea of George Washington at thirty" (p. 22).

She, in turn, is the object of his hopeless passion: "he adored her. He would willingly enough have damned himself for her. There was no sacrifice he would not have made to bring her nearer to him. In his upright, quiet, simple kind of way, he immolated himself before her" (p. 235). Yet, even though Mrs. Lee values the same things as he, to marry John Carrington would only reinforce her old ennui. Somehow at their age (she is thirty and he about forty) time has displaced them both. "I have done my best," she tells him, "to persuade myself that some day I might begin life again with the old hopes and feelings, but it is no use. The fire is burned out. If you married me, you would destroy yourself. You would wake up some day, and find the universe dust and ashes" (p. 261). Ten years before, Mrs. Lee thinks, she could have loved Carrington—a living Southern embodiment of her dead husband's aristocratic manner; but the Civil War and her husband's death have intervened in the meantime, and the world, as she tells him, will no longer "run as we want" (p. 236). Still, though they can not "begin life again" together as if nothing had changed, they are both preoccupied with memories and habits "belonging to an age already vanishing or vanished" (p. 217). Their common cause of "hunting for first principles" may have fallen irretrievably out of fashion, but they will continue their solemn "solitary struggle against fate" (p. 98). Neither will sacrifice, voluntarily, the "hopes and feelings" of the past that they know have been rendered obsolete by a changing postwar society.

Thus, aside from being a rival lover, the figure of Senator Ratcliffe represents a twofold threat for Carrington: at once moral and temporal. On the one hand, he violates every standard of honor and integrity that Carrington upholds; on the other hand, it is painfully clear to Carrington that the ability to "engineer" American society has passed into the hands of men like Ratcliffe, if it was not already there from the beginning of American history. Carrington's initial characterization of Ratcliffe to Mrs. Lee in the Senate chamber, for example, reflects his refined Southern aversion to "the Prairie Giant of Peonia":

> Can you see his eyes from here? I call them Yankee eyes. . . . Cold eyes, steel gray, rather small, not unpleasant in good-humour, diabolic in a passion, but worst when a little suspicious; then they watch you as though you were a young rattle-snake, to be killed when convenient. . . . His eyes only seem to ask the possible uses you might be put to. Ah, the vice-president has given him the floor; now we shall have it. Hard voice, is it not? like his eyes. Hard manner, like his voice. Hard all through. . . . Now he is settling down to his work. . . . See how he dodges all the sharp issues. What a thing it is to be a Yankee! What a genius the fellow has for leading a party! Do you see how well it is all done? The new President flattered and conciliated, the party united and given a strong lead. And now we shall see how the President will deal with him. Ten to one on Ratcliffe. Come, there is that stupid ass from Missouri getting up. Let us go (pp. 25, 26).

Adams skillfully infuses Carrington's description with a repressed bitterness and self-pity. And despite her own halfhearted defense of Yankees, Mrs. Lee also must eventually face the possibility that upsets Carrington, yet dissuades him at the same time from destroying Ratcliffe's public career when he later has the opportunity—the possibility, that is, that both power and history are on Ratcliffe's side. In their willing or unwilling attachment to the memories and habits that brought them together in the first place, Mrs. Lee and John Carrington are the impotent victims of time and tragedy. When one's experience and the source of one's security are thus negated or otherwise made obsolete, then one must either deny that fact by clinging to the past or adjust one's thought and behavior to the reality of a new and changing society.

For a while Mrs. Lee does both. She wants to embrace "the massive machinery of society" but, at the same time, keep her abstract principles of good and evil intact. She will accept and judge society only on her own terms; yet, once she has exposed herself to Ratcliffe's type and found herself "already deep in the mire of politics," she sees "how the great machine floundered about, bespattering with mud even her own pure garments" (p. 195). There is no question that Henry Adams wanted the reader of *Democracy* to condemn Ratcliffe as one of the chief disseminators of the political mud that soils the accustomed virtue of Mrs. Lee. For this, Ratcliffe is justly caned by that "impenetrable eighteenth-century cynic," Baron Jacobi, in the novel's final scene. Ratcliffe has no morals and, therefore, does not merit the reader's approval as a man. Yet it is equally clear that, in Adams's view, the loss of respectability, embodied in men like Ratcliffe, is one of the prices that a democratic society must pay for having a representative government:

> There may be some mistake about a doctrine which makes the wicked, when a majority, the mouthpiece of God against the virtuous, but the hopes of mankind are staked on it; and if the weak in faith sometimes quail when they see humanity floating in a shoreless ocean, on this plank, which experience and religion long since condemned as rotten, mistake or not, men have thus far floated better by its aid than the popes ever did with their prettier principles (p. 181).

Mrs. Lee is one of the virtuous who unfortunately must be sacrificed to "the hopes of mankind." But, in her case, the fact that she feels herself "los[ing] the distinction between right and wrong" in the course of the novel is not particularly significant; for someone else it might even have been a good thing (p. 199). Mrs. Lee, however, is also one of the "weak in faith" who quail when the reality of the political situation becomes too unbearable. She has reached an understanding of the incompatibility of political power and virtue only when it is too late. This is just another way of saying that, even if her own principles eventually lost their meaning, Mrs. Lee would still cling to them for self-defense. She can not sacrifice the habits of a lifetime. When she finally rejects Ratcliffe's proposal, the knowledge that he once accepted a $100,000 bribe is only an excuse, not a reason, for her action. Her decision, as she tells him, "is a very old one, . . . which I had let myself lose sight of, for a time" (p. 346).

Even though he overestimates his personal power, Ratcliffe still knows Mrs. Lee better than she knows herself; she is, and always will be, a "hard critic." "You judge," he says, "with the judgment of abstract principles, and you wield the bolts of divine justice. You look on and condemn, but you refuse to acquit" (p. 177). Perhaps Ratcliffe doesn't deserve acquittal; that, however, is not the point. Mrs. Lee would not have pardoned a lesser sinner or, especially, one who was less forthright than Ratcliffe.

It is, after all, to Ratcliffe's credit that he never attempts to conceal his own lack of principle; and it is to Mrs. Lee's discredit that she ignores his honesty. In his proposal of marriage, he makes his own character and philosophy perfectly clear: "I have done many things in my political career that are not defensible. To act with entire honesty and self-respect, one should always live in a pure atmosphere, and the atmosphere of politics is impure" (p. 309). This declaration can take Mrs. Lee by surprise only if she fails to recall his prior admission that he fixed an election for his party in Illinois during the war. But these revelations of Ratcliffe's moral weakness apparently fall on deaf ears or, perhaps, even increase Mrs. Lee's pity and philanthropy toward him. In this she only encourages him, until she finally realizes that to accept his offer of marriage would mean a sacrifice of her own self-control and her power over him. If she has made herself vulnerable to Ratcliffe, by clinging to the illusory relevance of her abstract principles, then she must somehow correct that situation and still retain her sense of superiority.

Mrs. Lee, primarily, is responsible for her nearly marrying someone she could never respect. After reading Carrington's revelation of Ratcliffe's betrayal of trust, the hardest thing for her to accept is "the discovery of her own weakness and self-deception" (p. 336). But once she has made this discovery, the problem is how to extricate herself while retaining some semblance of self-respect. Thus, she concludes that, if she had married Ratcliffe, she would not have lost entirely the ability to distinguish between right and wrong; her life would have been an "endless succession of moral somersaults," in which her ever-present conscience would have been stretched to its furthest limits, but never vanquished (p. 341). Fortunately, she thinks, she can avoid that eventuality, since she has already fulfilled her original purpose in coming to Washington:

> Had she not penetrated the deepest recesses of politics, and learned how easily the mere possession of power could convert the shadow of a hobby-horse exising only in the brain of a foolish country farmer, into a lurid nightmare that convulsed the sleep of nations? (p. 341).

Best of all, she had managed to learn this and still "had saved herself in time."

The question, however, that the reader of *Democracy* asks is whether Mrs. Lee has actually been able to preserve the viability of her virtue and principles. If it is too late for her to accept Ratcliffe's way of life, is it not also too late for her to deny some complicity in the strength and survival of his values (by refusing, with Carrington, to test those principles in public battle)? Is it the "sleep of nations" or her own sleep that has been convulsed by the "lurid nightmare" of American politics? By taking comfort from the fact that politicians were, in reality, as bad as her common sense might have told her, is she not retreating to the moral safety of her original sense of superiority? She would like to believe that being married to Silas P. Ratcliffe would have been a continual moral crisis, but what really frightens her is the thought that she might indeed have changed and come down to his level—that she just might have been "of use in the world" (p.

340). If it was politics that had caused "this atrophy of the moral senses by disuse" (p. 353) in Ratcliffe, could the same thing not happen to her as his wife?

Surely Mrs. Lee is correct when she tells Ratcliffe that "we are not fitted for each other. Our lives run in separate grooves" (p. 347). But the grooves she speaks of are as much psychological and social as they are moral, and Ratcliffe, it should be said, knows this. Thus, when he insists that "there is no such divergence in our lives," he is only stating the practical truth that there need not be one if she marries him. This idea understandably upsets Mrs. Lee, and she again asserts that "you and I take very different views of life" (p. 347). But it is clear, by this time, that the difference between her attitudes and his is a question of desire as well as habit. She is, above all, afraid of herself—afraid that, even with her stubborn moral principles, she is not strong enough (her word is *competent*) to reform in any way the impure atmosphere of politics or even to put her principles to the test. That would tangle her life too much. It is much safer for her, morally and psychologically, to return to her old philanthropic ways in New York City, where she can stand in judgment over American politics from a purer social atmosphere. As R.P. Balckmur has put it, *Democracy*

> shows the intelligence which is willing to tamper with the actual without being willing to seize it, as properly humiliated and sent flying. If the failure of [Mrs. Lee] lay deeper than that, it was perhaps that she never understood the principle that the intelligence must always act as if it were adequate to the problems it has aroused. That is, it must see the evils it attacks as the vivid forms of its own abused and debased self. Otherwise, it must give up.[5]

"What rest it would be," Madeleine exclaims after Ratcliffe has departed, "to live in the Great Pyramid and look out for ever at the polar star!" (p. 370).

The irony of the final pages of *Democracy* is that the rest Mrs. Lee is seeking may really be the "death in life" that Ratcliffe vainly tried to persuade her against—a secure, aristocratic manner of living in which she can shelter herself and her principles—"like a saint on a solitary column" (p. 362)—from the convulsions of American democracy. And this fate would be no less probable if John Carrington, on Mrs. Lee's sister's recommendation, did "try again" and married Mrs. Lee when she returned from her hasty escape to Europe. Both of them have abandoned American politics to the Ratcliffes, and, together, they could have shared the rather self-righteous consolation of her final postscript to him: "nine out of ten of our country men would say I had made a mistake" (p. 374). So history continues to move onward without Madeleine Lee.

4

"Hurried particles in the stream": Henry James's *The Bostonians*

Henry James's *The Bostonians* is, in many ways, remarkably similar to the two novels that immediately precede and follow it in this discussion of social change and nostalgia.[1] Lily Bart in *The House of Mirth*, Madeleine Lee, and Olive Chancellor are all searching, in their separate situations, for a stable style of life that will give them a twofold assurance of social distinction and personal self-control. One of the alternative systems of habits and manners offered to them and, in varying degrees and for varying reasons, rejected by them is represented by the historical conservatism of John Carrington, Basil Ransom, and Lawrence Selden. The women attempt, unsuccessfully, to adjust to a public life characterized by social change; the men seek to preserve a private life of order and permanence. But either course of action is inevitably misguided and joyless, for, as Irving Howe put the issue in reference to *The Bostonians*, "no distinction can finally be made between public and private experience, so that the deformations of one soon become the deformations of the other."[2] Thus, the treatment of character in these novels closely approximates what James considered the greatest virtue of his master,

75

Turgenev: the "ironic" and "tender" vision of the individual figure

> with its minutest signs and tricks—all its heredity of idiosyncrasies, all its particular weakness and strength, of ugliness and beauty, of oddity and charm; and yet it is of [Turgenev's] essence that he sees it in the general flood of life, steeped in its relations and contacts, struggling or submerged, a hurried particle in the stream.[3]

Basil Ransom and Olive Chancellor are indeed "hurried particles in the stream," "struggling" against the threat of insignificance and obsolescence in the historical "flood" of American society. In a word, they are both *provincials.* Ransom, for example, has fled from a "blighted South" to the greener financial pastures of New York City. Like John Carrington, he is a member of the "dilapidated gentry" who fought and suffered in a losing cause during the "immense national fiasco" of the Civil War. But, in escaping his defeated culture, Ransom has by no means abandoned his lifelong habits of thought; in fact, the only kind of success he can imagine for himself in the North is one based upon the conservatism that insulates him from the historical crisis and shock of the war. Consequently, after failing as a practical lawyer, he vainly attempts to make an adequate living by publishing reactionary essays in obscure periodicals, such as the *Rational Review.* From that rostrum he can safely decry the growing chaos of American society and, in particular, the increasingly popular cause of female suffrage. He is, as James describes him, "much addicted to judging his age."

> He thought it talkative, querulous, hysterical, maudlin, full of false ideas, of unhealthy germs, of extravagant, dissipated habits, for which a great reckoning was in store. He was an immense admirer of the late Thomas Carlyle, and was very suspicious of the encroachments of modern democracy.[4]

"The whole generation," Ransom tells the astounded Verena Tarrant in Central Park, "is womanised";

the masculine tone is passing out of the world; it's a feminine, a nervous, hysterical, chattering, canting age, an age of hollow phrases and false delicacy and exaggerated solicitudes and coddled sensibilities, which, if we don't soon look out, will usher in the reign of mediocrity, of the feeblest and flattest and the most pretentious that has ever been. The masculine character, the ability to dare and endure, to know and yet not fear reality, to look the world in the face and take it for what it is—a very queer and partly very base mixture—that is what I want to preserve, or rather, as I may say, to recover; and I must tell you that I don't in the least care what becomes of you ladies while I make the attempt! (pp. 333–34).

Women, after all, "were essentially inferior to men, and infinitely tiresome when they declined to accept the lot which men had made for them" (pp. 192–93); they ought to have been "private and passive, and have no feeling but for that," and to have left "any responsibility for the government of the world" to "the sex of tougher hide" (p. 11). Unfortunately for Ransom, ideas such as these seem, to the prospective publishers of the 1870s, to be "three hundred years behind the age"—the doctrines of "some transmitted spirit of a robust but narrow ancestor, some broadfaced wig-wearer or sword-bearer, with a more primitive conception of manhood than our modern temperament appears to require" (p. 190).

These doctrines, however, despite their ineffectuality, are not wholly deprecated by James, whose confessed purpose in *The Bostonians* was to depict the most "peculiar" aspect of American society—"the decline of the sentiment of sex."[5] The fact that Ransom is predisposed to have certain beliefs that appear incongruous outside his own culture is both understandable and forgivable as James portrays it. It is, instead, not so much *what* Ransom thinks as *how* he thinks—his inflexible romanticism—that draws the irony of his author. Because Ransom is a representative of a "fallen aristocracy" who has come north to live in the center of an industrial democracy, the intensity of his beliefs is a measure of the degree to which they function as a defense mechanism to be clung to until, as he hopes, "the slow process, the sensible beneficence, of time" (p. 50) will gradually ease the pain of his nostalgia for the old, pre-Civil War South. Of course, the irony here—the first of many in *The Bostonians*—is that Ransom has fled from the one society where the passage of time might resemble the slow process he desires; in the urban centers of the North, on the other hand, time seems to move at too great a speed for Ransom's comfort. Thus, as the novel progresses, his thinking becomes more and more inflexible, and, though he is the only "victor" in the final chapter, Ransom is nevertheless a prime example of Irving Howe's conclusion that "the price of a complex civilization is often the complex diminution of pleasure."[6]

The Northern "civilization" into which Ransom comes with "an immense desire for success" (p. 17) is indeed a "complex" one for him in two important ways. Not only has he left the South for a new, more affluent environment, but the character of Northern society in which he seeks to make a living has itself radically changed from its prewar days. Whereas, in *Democracy,* it was Mrs. Lee who altered her accustomed environment and Carrington who most experienced the psychological crisis of the Civil War, in *The Bostonians,* it is Basil Ransom who assumes both these burdens. Surely much of the complexity he witnesses in the Northern cities is physical in nature, the result of an inexorable industrial revolution; as he gazes out the window of Olive Chancellor's apartment overlooking the Charles River, for example, he sees "an horizon indented at empty intervals with wooden spires, the masts of lonely boats, the chimneys of dirty 'works,' over a brackish expanse of anomalous character, which is too big for a river and too small for a bay" (p. 15)—the same "desolate" view of "sordid tubes of factories and engine-shops" (p. 174) that James later describes in contrast to the hermetically sealed intensity of Olive's and Verena's cause. But the poverty of this scene does not seem to affect Ransom and the two reformers: he thinks it rather "picturesque" and "romantic," while Olive and Verena either ignore it or rejoice in the "loveliness" of the setting sun that obscures the meanness of the reality below. Nor does Ransom appear to be upset by his degenerate surroundings in New York City, a neighborhood that "was fatal to any pretensions Ransom and his fellow-lodgers might have had in regard to gentility of situation" (p. 185).

The conclusion that James seems to wish the reader to draw from his characters' obliviousness to the decaying environment around them is simply that reality, for Basil Ransom and Olive Chancellor in particular, is essentially psychological rather than physical. Thus, their ideas—as mutually antipathetic as they may be—serve the same purpose in each case of shielding the character from the harsher facts of historical change and human need. James's comment that "history seemed . . . in every way horrible" to Olive and Verena (p. 175) has a further significance that applies to Ransom as well. In truth, both he and Olive are "behind the age" in their thinking, even though the cause that she supports is one of "the encroachments of modern democracy" that Ransom abhors.

In Ransom's case, the unpopularity of his ideas only increases his desire to take possession of Verena Tarrant. To gain complete mastery over her would not only be a living proof of the viability of his ideas, despite their unpopularity, but would also be a way, for Ransom, of reversing the momentum of history and retrieving an old antebellum image of feminine purity and innocence:

> He didn't care for her engagements, her campaigns, or all the expectancy of her friends; to "squelch" all that, at a stroke, was the dearest wish of his heart. It would represent to him his own success, it would symbolise his victory. It became a fixed idea with him, and he warned her again and again. . . . He felt almost capable of kidnapping her. It was palpably in the air that she would become "widely popular," and that idea simply sickened him (p. 393).

Inevitably, Ransom does win his battle with Olive because Verena happens to be the right kind of woman; it is "in her nature to be easily submissive, to like being overborne" (p. 328). And, as Olive fears, Ransom is accordingly filled with "joy and elation" at "this illustrious, consummate proof of the fickleness, the futility, the predestined servility, of women" (p. 379). Of course, Verena is no such proof, however she may serve to soothe his ego temporarily. Ransom's success with her justifies his obsolete theories as little as the one essay in the *Rational Review* justifies his dream of fame and fortune. As the last ironic lines of the novel indicate, after he has "rescued" the sobbing Verena from Olive Chancellor, the position of such a man is historically beyond repair: "It is to be feared that with the union, so far from brilliant, into which she was about to enter, these were not the last [tears] she was destined to shed" (p. 449).

In one sense, Ransom's chief victim in *The Bostonians,* Olive Chancellor, does stand at the opposite pole from him. She is a reformer and has thrown herself into the modern movement for women's suffrage. Yet Olive's desire to possess Verena is, in its own way, just as much related to social position and lifelong habits of thought as is Ransom's; both of them need Verena to reaffirm a heroic style of life that, they feel, has been lost in the postwar frenzy and commercialism of American society. For Olive, who has been brought up in Boston—"the city of reform"—the need to feel attuned to a heroic time in history is reflected in her unbounded desire to be a martyr in a truly unpopular cause—as the early abolitionists had to be in their day and age. In those times, it seems to her, the reform movement was motivated by a selflessness that had been lost with its increase in popularity. Since the end of the war, the element of self-sacrifice had been compromised by considerations of comfort and self-interest, a situation that is revealed in Olive's own nostalgia for a purer age of reform. Miss Chancellor, James says,

> would have been much happier if the movements she was interested in could have been carried on only by the people she liked, and if revolutions, somehow, didn't always have to begin with one's self—with internal convulsions, sacrifices, executions. A common end, unfortunately, however fine as regards a special result, does not make community impersonal (p. 111).

In particular, Olive's nostalgia accounts for the bitter inspiration she feels when she is around the "original" and "deliciously provincial" Miss Birdseye:

> She had always had for Olive a kind of aroma of martyrdom and her battered, unremunerated, unpensioned old age brought angry tears, springing from depths of outraged theory, into Miss Chancellor's eyes. . . . Olive would have liked to hang [her old-fashioned weapons] up as venerable relics of a patient fight, and this was what she seemed to do when she made the poor lady relate her battles—never glorious and brilliant, but obscure and wastefully heroic—call back the figures of her companions in arms, exhibit her medals and scars (pp. 179, 178).

Of course, part of Olive's affection for Miss Birdseye is the pity she feels for "a representative of suffering humanity"; but she also pities herself and envies the woman who "never, in her long, unrewarded, weary life, had a thought or an impulse for herself" (p. 37). Devoid of vanity or self-consciousness, Miss Birdseye is indeed "the last link in a tradition," whose death would terminate "the heroic age of New England life—the age of plain living and high thinking, of pure ideals and earnest effort, of moral passion and noble experiment" (p. 179). That age is gone, and Olive knows it. She need only observe the Tarrants, Farrinders, and Burrages—and herself—to see that the qualities of "plain living," "high thinking," "pure ideals," "earnest effort," "moral passion," and "noble experiment" have all become alloys of the original. Since the war, the cause of reform has been appropriated by the self-server and dubious believer. Olive would like to think that she is not one of these, but the fact that she is essentially preoccupied with the "romance of the people," and not the physical reality of the poverty and meanness around her, gives her away. She can readily perceive the Tarrants' "vulgar exploitation" of Verena for prestige and publicity, the comfortable, blasé patronage of the Burrages, and the commercial public relations of Mrs. Farrinder, but she can not face the possibility that the passage of time has distorted and perverted her own ideals. Psychologically, Olive is guilty of the same offense she attributes to the wealthy Mrs. Burrage: living and fattening "on abuses, prejudices, privileges, on the petrified, cruel fashions of the past" (p. 305). She is proud of her own social position in Boston—a kind of ideological, rather than financial, upper class—and is annoyed at Mrs. Farrinder's inability to make the distinction:

> She knew her place in the Boston hierarchy, and it was not what Mrs. Farrinder supposed; so that there was a want of perspective in talking to her as if she had been a representative of the aristocracy. Nothing could be weaker, she knew very well, than (in the United States) to apply that term too literally; nevertheless, it would represent a reality if one were to say that, by distinction, the Chancellors belonged to the bourgeoisie—the oldest and best (p. 34).

But the distinction Olive cherishes is no longer relevant to the success of the postwar reform movement—her form of aristocracy is as obsolete as Ransom's. In Miss Birdseye's day, moral prestige may have been inseparable from power, ideas from action; but in the 1870s, as James describes them, the increased popularity of social reform precludes a heroic dimension to personal conduct and fosters both the creation of new "types" (the Burrages) and the degradation of old (the Tarrants). Olive's wealth, in turn, becomes an asset to the movement and a hindrance to her dreams of martyrdom. She is embarrassed when Ranson, at their first meeting, declares that "I would change my position for yours any day. That's what I said to myself as I sat there in your elegant home." "She disliked," says James, "to be reminded of certain things which, for her, were mitigations of the hard feminine lot" (p. 24). What galls Olive the most is that women evidently do not "suffer" as much as they did in Miss Birdseye's day. Her own material comfort, in a large measure, denies her that privilege; and, because affluence itself has become an inescapable psychological condition in postwar American society, Olive is the frustrated victim of her own age. She can not finally sacrifice her economic position because her cultural distinction, which is protected by wealth, is even more precious to her than her moral ideals: "in a career in which she was constantly exposing herself to offense and laceration, her most poignant suffering came from the injury of her taste"(p. 29).

In contrast to the conscious "culture" of Olive's life (the "organized privacy," for example, that Ransom feels in her city house with "so many objects that spoke of habits and tastes" [p. 16]), the "bareness" of Miss Birdseye's "long, loose, empty parlour . . . told that she had never had any needs but moral needs, and that all her history had been that of her sympathies" (p. 29)—something that could never have been said of Olive Chancellor. For years, James says, Olive herself

> had been active enough . . . in the city-missions; she too had scoured dirty children, and, in squalid lodging-houses, had gone into rooms where the domestic situation was strained and the noises made the neighbours turn pale. But she reflected that after such exertions she had the refreshment of a pretty house, a drawing-room full of flowers, a crackling hearth, where she threw in pine-cones and made them snap, an imported tea-service, a Chickering piano, and the *Deutsche Rundschau;* whereas Miss Birdseye had only a bare, vulgar room, with a hideous flowered carpet (it looked like a dentist's), a cold furnace, the evening paper, and Doctor Prance (p. 180).

It is this kind of physical "vulgarity" that Olive can not tolerate for herself, despite the embarrassment she feels over her own affluence and comfort; above all, she despises the personal vulgarity that is embodied in Verena's parents and rewarded in the cause of reform. Yet, at the same time, Olive is willing to buy off the Tarrants and exploit their naturally theatrical daughter for her own purposes. The painful truth is that, with the single exception of the "impersonal" Miss Birdseye, every one of the reformers, vulgar or not, is concerned with personal appearance and social position; even the innocent Verena has been trained to perform.

In Olive Chancellor, what Lionel Trilling called *pride of class*—based on "the ability to fight and administer"—has become *snobbery*—"pride in status without pride in function." This, according to Trilling, is "the peculiar vice not of aristocratic societies which have their own appropriate vices, but of bourgeois democratic societies"—exactly the kind of society in which Olive imagines herself to be one of the "oldest and best." The dominant emotions of snobbery—"uneasiness, self-consciousness, self-defensiveness, the sense that one is not quite real but can in some way acquire reality"[7]—are the qualities that make Olive's nature "like a skiff in a stormy sea." In this situation, therefore, the greater the power she can exert over Verena, the greater is her "sense of security" (p. 146). She thinks that, by imposing on Verena "an effectual rupture with her past" (p. 109), she can preserve in herself the social distinction of a heroic life—her own romantic link with the past. Like Madeleine Lee, Olive is engaged in a love-hate relationship with American society: she wants to "learn" without sacrificing either her "lofty principles" or her social position. "I want to give myself up to others," she says; "I want to know everything that lies beneath and out of sight, don't you know?" (p. 36). But this gesture of self-sacrifice is, in the last analysis, a kind of inverted snobbishness. By thriving on what is "common," her own sense of personal power and social importance is reinforced. Thus she exults in the fact that it was impossible for Verena

> to have had an origin less distinguished than Tarrant himself. His birth, in some unheard-of place in Pennsylvania, was quite inexpressibly low, and Olive would have been much disappointed if it had been wanting in this defect. She liked to think that Verena, in her childhood, had known almost the extremity of poverty, and there was a kind of ferocity in the joy with which she reflected that there had been moments when this delicate creature came near (if the pinch had only lasted a little longer) to literally going without food (pp. 109–110).

For all her dreams of martyrdom, Olive really wants to suffer vicariously—to embrace, and yet protect herself from, "the social dusk of that mysterious democracy" that Verena seems to represent (p. 79).

To differentiate between Olive's private and public motives for wanting to possess Verena is, in the end, a pointless task; whatever abnormality exists in her character is merely a symptom of the abnormality and tensions of her society and the consequent discrepancy between its reality and her illusions. She is as much a victim of a complex civilization as Ransom; history has made her dreams as obsolete as his. For her to ask Verena why Ranson would choose her from "among all the exposed millions of our sex, . . . when everything he knew about you showed you to be, exactly, the very last" (p. 378) is a final revelation of Olive's self-deception and desperation. The answer, of course, is that Verena is not "meant" for anything except to be controlled by a stronger will than her own. What attracts Olive to her is the same thing that attracts Ransom: her childlike weakness. Ransom wins Verena simply because his is a theory of weakness, and Olive's is not.

Yet even though Ransom wins, as he must, he is no less self-deceived than Olive. If she is blind to the nature of her own motives, he is blind to the worth of his. Like John Carrington in *Democracy,* he dreams of heroically rescuing the innocent damsel from an evil society:

> [Verena] was a touching, ingenuous victim, unconscious of the pernicious forces which were hurrying her to her ruin. With this idea of ruin there had already associated itself in the young man's mind, the idea . . . of rescue; and it was the disposition to confirm himself in the view that her charm was her own, and her fallacies, her absurdity, a mere reflection of unlucky circumstance, that led him to make an effort to behold her in the position in which he could least bear to think of her (p. 247).

With this in mind, it is worth noticing that, in the final chapters of the novel, Ransom becomes obsessed with the idea of rescuing Verena and finally breaks her will at the obscure hamlet of Marmion on Cape Cod, which seems to have been bypassed by the mainstream of contemporary society. There, where the abandoned shipyards give him the "impression of fallen greatness," the feeling that the village "had had a larger life, seen better days," he is much more at home, his confidence revived (p. 352). Even the old reformer, Miss Birdseye, whose heroic past appeals to Ransom for some of the same reasons it appeals to Olive, has similar feelings about Marmion:

> I enjoy everything in this little old-world place; I didn't suppose I should be satisfied to be so passive. It's a great contrast to my former exertions. But somehow it doesn't seem as if there were any trouble or any wrong round here (p. 362).

If Ransom and his commandeered bride could make their future home in a place like this, then perhaps his dream of a heroic rescue might become a reality, and perhaps her final tears would indeed be "the last she was destined to shed." But Ransom can not escape into the past, nor even live an "old-world place" like Marmion; his honor and ambition demand that he be a financial success. He will, of course, fail, and his "castles in the air" —because they are exactly that—will come tumbling down, as surely as Olive's dreams of power and prestige.

The moral of the story, as in *Democracy,* is simply the ironic futility of aristocratic illusions in a changing society. Though Ransom wins the battle, he loses the war. Despite his "deep aversion for the ineffectual" (p. 17), his own ideas are powerless. And, though Olive is defeated, the historical forces with which she has aligned herself, for whatever reasons, will ultimately be victorious. Ransom's final conquest is only a Pyrrhic victory, for if Verena's choice, as Irving Howe has stated, is "in accordance with those rhythms of life which Olive bluntly violates but Ransom merely exploits,"[8] it is equally clear that Ranson is further removed from the *rhythms of history* than is the cause that Olive represents. The very fact that, in *The Bostonians,* the "rhythms of life" are sometimes at odds with the "rhythms of history" is the hallmark of a changing society that must inevitably withhold from Olive Chancellor and Basil Ransom the satisfaction of their desires and the fulfillment of their dreams.

5

"The whirling surface of existence": Edith Wharton's
The House of Mirth

The dramatic situation of Lily Bart, the beautiful and charming "heroine" of Edith Wharton's *The House of Mirth,* is comparable to the central dramatic situation in *The Bostonians.* Olive Chancellor would like to relive the heroic age of the early abolitionists; and Lily similarly yearns for a social community that is at once "impersonal" and "noble," a world in which her own distinction is an integral part of a larger whole. "The life she longed to lead," Mrs. Wharton says, was "the life of fastidious aloofness and refinement in which every detail should have the finish of a jewel. and the whole form a harmonious setting to her own jewel-like rareness."[1] No such world exists, however, for either Lily Bart or the less "rare" Olive Chancellor. Rather, the social milieu of New York in the first decade of the twentieth century and of Boston in the 1870s share the same historical characteristics: impermanence, unpredictability, and insecurity. The "social fluctuations," which Lily's Aunt Peniston faithfully records from the window of her Fifth Avenue apartment, are "the distinguishing features of each season." Below her pass the "new people" who "rose to the surface with each recurring tide, and were either submerged beneath its rush or landed triumphantly beyond the reach of envious breakers" (p. 193). Even for those members of the nouveau riche who momentarily gain the notoriety and envy that comes with wealth, vicissitudes always remain. Mrs. Peniston "was apt to display a remarkable retrospective insight into [the] ultimate fate [of these people], so that, when they had fulfilled their destiny, she was almost always able to say to Grace Stepney—the recipient of her prophesies —that she had known exactly what would happen" (p. 193). In essence, the society that Edith Wharton has Mrs. Peniston observe "from the secluded watch-tower of her upper window" is not unlike the kind of "republican country" with its "fluctuating waves" of social life that Hawthorne described in *The House of the Seven Gables,* or the "democratic" society that de Tocqueville identified by its constantly rising and falling families.[2] When the "track of generations" has been effaced and "the reverence that belonged to what is old has vanished," de Tocqueville concluded,

> birth, condition, and profession no longer distinguish men, or scarcely distinguish them; hardly anything but money remains to create strongly marked differences between them and to raise some of them above the common level.[3]

Lily Bart is surrounded by people who are struggling to raise themselves, financially and therefore socially, "above the common level." Some are more obvious, or honest, about their aspirations than others (Simon Rosedale, the Jewish businessman, for example), but all march, in the end, to the same tune. The various "sets" with which Lily is associated in the course of the novel—the Trenors and their "house of mirth" on Long Island, the Dorsets, Brys, Gormers, and Mrs. Hatch—are all cut from the same cloth: they all want to be "the most important people in sight." Therefore, whoever is above someone else on the scale of wealth and notoriety becomes, on the one hand, a competitor and, on the other hand, the one who establishes the accepted standard of conduct. Such a situation, as Lily discovers, was not unlike "a play of party politics, in which every concession had its recognized equivalent" (p. 417). Self-interest, not principle, was the controlling factor; it all came back to the equation of "influence" and "the power of money" (p. 421).

Lily's story begins with a week's visit to Bellomont—the house of the novel's title. There, in its "tumultuous disorder," she feels the kind of security that comes with anonymity: "no one seemed to have time to observe any one else, and private aims and personal interests were swept along unheeded in the rush of collective activities" (pp. 368–69). Having been raised by an ambitious mother to value luxury, Lily is, to some extent, at home at Bellomont. "She was not made," she thinks to herself, "for mean and shabby surroundings, for the squalid compromises of poverty. Her whole being dilated in an atmosphere of luxury; it was the background she required, the only climate she could breathe in" (pp. 39–40). The luxury provided by others, however, is not what Lily Bart basically needs or wants. At age twenty-nine, she is still single and beginning "to feel herself a mere pensioner on the splendour which had once seemed to belong to her" (p. 40); yet, even when she tries to accept and keep pace with that "splendour," the "laws of the universe" appear "to leave her out of its calculations" (p. 42). At Bellomont, in particular, Lily must not only maintain a high standard of living, with the help of her aunt's patronage, but must also participate in the bridge games that, like a vicious circle, merely deplete the funds that qualify her to play in the first place. Her beauty, of course, is an important factor in her social acceptance; but, beauty or not, she must continually please her hostesses, and playing cards is "one of the taxes she had to pay for their prolonged hospitality" (p. 41). When she does win at bridge, she imprudently spends the money on more clothes and jewelry, instead of saving it to offset future losses. When she loses, on the other hand, the gambling passion overtakes her, and she increases her bets. By thus subjecting herself to "the terrible gods of chance," Lily tries to stay afloat in a society that is far more competitive than it is communal. The "rush of collective activities" is not the kind of security that Lily needs.

More money will not solve her problem. In reality, it is freedom from the concern with money, rather than money per se, that fires her imagination—precisely the style of life and manner of thinking that is nowhere to be found in the "great social machine" that seems to imprison her. Lily's own preference would have been for a more "picturesque" community,

> for an English nobleman with political ambitions and vast estates; or, for second choice, an Italian prince with a castle in the Apennines and an hereditary office in the Vatican. Lost causes had a romantic charm for her, and she liked to picture herself as standing aloof from the vulgar press of the Quirinal, and sacrificing her pleasure to the claims of an immemorial tradition (p. 55).

But these visions are doomed to frustration in a society whose safest refuge from "the vulgar press of the Quirinal" is the "house of mirth" itself. History has permanently relegated to the past any semblance of "immemorial tradition," if it ever existed in America in the first place.

For a while, Lily's instinctive social needs do seem to be satisfied at Bellomont; Mrs. Trenor appears to be the kind of disinterested patron who might relieve Lily's deepest and most honorable anxieties by providing her with a stable, impersonal community:

> [Judy Trenor] could not sustain life except in a crowd. The collective nature of her interests exempted her from the ordinary rivalries of her sex, and she knew no more personal emotion than that of hatred for the woman who presumed to give bigger dinners or have more amusing house-parties than herself. . . . In Miss Bart's utilitarian classification of her friends, Mrs. Trenor ranked as the woman who was least likely to "go back" on her (pp. 63–64).

But the impersonality of Bellomont is, in the end, all surface, masking a more fundamental state of incoherence and insecurity; its virtue lies only in the fact that its "machinery" was "so carefully concealed that one scene flow[ed] into another without perceptible agency" (p. 487). It is a "giant gilt cage" that confronts Lily with the prospect of "servitude to the whims of others, never the possibility of asserting her own eager individuality"

(p. 162). She can not, in short, have both the "larger whole" and the sense of personal distinction that she desires.

Lily's eventual exclusion from the house of mirth is the result, quite appropriately, of the stock market—the one institution that is responsible for virtually everyone's social fate in *The House of Mirth*. The market, however, is not merely the modus operandi of this society; in Edith Wharton's hands it becomes a central metaphor for the inescapable capriciousness of American social history. At one point in the novel, for example, the author comments that

> it had been a bad autumn in Wall Street, where prices fell in accordance with that perculiar law which proves railway stocks and bales of cotton to be more sensitive to the allotment of executive power than many estimable citizens trained to all the advantages of self-government. Even fortunes supposed to be independent of the market either betrayed a secret dependence on it, or suffered from a sympathetic affection: fashion sulked in its country-houses, or came to town incognito, general entertainments were discountenanced, and informality and short dinners became the fashion.
>
> But society, amused for a while at playing Cinderella, soon wearied of the hearthside role, and welcomed the Fairy God-mother in the shape of any magician powerful enough to turn the shrunken pumpkin back again into the golden coach. The mere fact of growing richer at a time when most people's investments are shrinking, is calculated to attract envious attention (p. 194).

It is to this "vast mysterious Wall Street world of 'tips' and 'deals' " that Lily turns to save her social position at Bellomont when her debts begin to surpass her aunt's gifts of money. After a little of her feminine persuasion, Gus Trenor offers to invest some money for her without endangering her already depleted funds. For her part, Lily "understood only that her modest investments were to be mysteriously multiplied without risk to herself; and the assurance that this miracle would take place within a short time, that there would be no tedious interval for suspense and reaction, relieved her of her lingering scruples" (p. 136). She accepts Trenor's offer and shortly thereafter receives her first thousand-dollar check in the mail. Eight thousand more comes later before Trenor himself is "heavily 'touched' " by the fall in stocks. Lily assumes that Trenor borrowed on her securities to raise the initial sum; but all her acquaintances seem to be aware of the fact, before she, that he has really been "paying her bills" with his own money. Only after it becomes clear—when he contrives to be alone with her at his house in the city—that he wants some affection in return for his generosity does Lily finally realize the nature of her debt to him. And when Mrs. Trenor learns the truth, she publicly rebuffs her former "friend"; if Judy was careless of her husband's affections, Lily thinks, "she was plainly jealous of his pocket" (p. 369).

The fact of her debt to Gus Trenor drives Lily, in book two of *The House of Mirth,* into the arms of other aspirants to the Trenors' social position. Initially, as "an almost miraculous release from crushing difficulties," she receives an invitation from the Dorsets to go abroad with them (p. 314). Lily, however, is destined to be used and abused by her friends as long as she remains single. Her job with the Dorsets is simply to distract George Dorset's attention from this wife Bertha's affair with a much younger man, for which services Lily receives "three months of luxury and freedom from care." Eventually, when George becomes suspicious and angry, it is Lily who is sacrificed: in order to make her husband think she is jealous, Bertha calmly lets it be known that Lily is trying to marry George, and then dismisses Lily from her company in Europe. The moral of the episode is expressed earlier in the novel by another character:

> When a girl's as good-looking as that she'd better marry; then no questions are asked. In our imperfectly organized society there is no provision as yet for the young woman who claims the privileges of marriage without assuming its obligations (p. 254).

Of course, Lily has not "claimed" the privileges of marriage either in reference to Gus Trenor or George Dorset, at least not knowingly. But she has been naive in attempting to maintain the habit of luxury without relying solely on the income of a guardian or a husband. And she will not accept the "obligations" that come with a society that falls short of her dreams.

It is also true, however, that Lily Bart remains a totally social creature: "if [she] were not a part of the season's fixed routine, [she] swung unsphered in a void of social non-existence"; and Lily, "for all her dissatisfied dreaming, had never really conceived the possibility of revolving about a different centre: it was easy enough to despise the world, but decidedly difficult to find any other habitable region" (p. 421). Thus, after Bertha Dorset's accusations, which lead, in turn, to Mrs. Peniston's disinheritance of her niece, Lily must "set out to regain, little by little, the position she had lost" (p. 366). This means, in lieu of Bellomont, "being of importance among the insignificant," as she had been earlier with the Wellington Brys (among the few people who noticeably benefit from the stock market in *The House of Mirth*). If those people welcomed her presence, "it proved that she was still conspicuous in the world to which they aspired" (p. 181). And, indeed, as long as people like the Brys remain "insignificant" in New York social circles, Lily's presence does give them prestige; but as the Brys's reputation rises, in the course of the novel, Lily's falls, and they snub her as quickly as they once deferred to her.

After her disinheritance, the situation is the same. She becomes involved with the Sam Gormers, who, even though they are "getting on a good deal faster than the Brys," are again among the insignificant by Lily's standards—a "social out-skirt which Lily had always fastidiously avoided" (p. 376). The crowds at the Gormers's parties, it seems to her, "were doing the same things as the Trenors, the Van Osburghs, and the Dorsets," but with less restraint; and "instead of shrinking from her as her own friends had done, they received her without question into the easy promiscuity of their lives" (pp. 376, 377). "As became persons of their rising consequence," however, the Gormers were also building a country house on Long Island. And with the first visit from their neighbor, Bertha Dorset, Lily becomes conscious "of a change in the relation between Mattie [Gormer] and herself, of a dawning discrimination, a gradually formed social standard, emerging from Mrs. Gormer's chaotic view of life" (p. 420).

Lily, in the end, is—at least financially—her own worst enemy, since she refuses to compromise her moral values to achieve her social aspirations: she declines to marry Simon Rosedale, but, more important, she declines to use Bertha Dorset's love letters to Lawrence Selden as a form of retribution for Bertha's malice toward her. Yet Selden, whose affection for Lily might seem to represent her only possible escape from "the great social machine," is himself unable to rescue her. Though he thinks that "he could never be a factor in her calculations," he is still attracted to her, partly out of pity for her as a "victim of the civilization which had produced her" (pp. 8, 10), and partly out of admiration for the "streak of sylvan freedom in her nature" (p. 19)—that quality which makes her seem at times to "despise the things she's trying for" (p. 303). For her part, Lily finds in him what she most wants to experience in life: "the air of belonging to a more specialized race, of carrying the impress of a concentrated past" (p. 104).

Nevertheless, despite their honest feelings for each other, neither of them is ever able to break with the past. As a young lawyer with an "aristocratic" background, Selden has inherited a "detachment from the sumptuary side of life: the Stoic's carelessness of material things, combined with the Epicurean's pleasure in them" (p. 246). He reflects his parents' love of "restraint and discrimination," a manner of living in which the most dangerous pitfall is the kind of "aimless profusion" that seems to characterize Lily's struggle with the material world. On the one hand, Selden forces Lily to face the reality of her character—the presence within her, as Edith Wharton says, of "two beings, one drawing deep breaths of freedom and exhilaration, the other gasping for air in a little black prison-house of fears" (p. 102). On the other hand, Selden can not satisfy the yearnings he arouses in her. He prides himself on remaining "amphibious," as he puts it, between the realm of wealth and his own "republic of the spirit," and he refuses to risk his equilibrium by sympathizing completely with Lily's plight. In the last analysis, he fears her material ambitions more than he loves her vitality and passion; it is much simpler for him to judge Lily

> by her habitual conduct than by the rare deviations from it which had thrown her so disturbingly in his way; and every act of hers which made the recurrence of such deviations more unlikely, confirmed the sense of relief with which he returned to the conventional view of her (p. 438).

"Why do you make the things I have chosen seem hateful to me," Lily cries, "if you have nothing to give me instead. . . . For all your fine phrases you're really as great a coward as I am" (pp. 114, 116). And, to the degree to which he means "to keep free from permanent ties" (p. 244), he is a coward.

But Selden's failure is as inevitable as it is willful. At the heart of his "spiritual fastidiousness" and ineffectuality is an aristocratic fatalism that would deny, to begin with, his ability to help Lily. When she challenges his "republic of the spirit" as a "close corporation," he absolves himself of responsibility ("It is not *my* republic") and meekly concludes that, "No, I have nothing to give you," as an alternative to the house of mirth and its imitators (pp. 113, 115). Selden does not want to have to work at love and thus endanger the safety of his "republic":

> he could vividly conceive of a love which should broaden and deepen till it became the central fact of life. What he could not accept, in his own case, was the makeshift alternative of a relation that should be less than this: that should leave some portions of his nature unsatisfied, while it put an undue strain on others. He would not, in other words, yield to the growth of an affection which might appeal to pity yet leave the understanding untouched (p. 246).

Nor, in fact, would he yield to an affair with Lily Bart that would surely appeal to *both* his pity and his understanding. Selden is simply a living testimony to the inevitable death of aristocratic values in a democratic society: the refusal to compromise the noble life when it ceases to be viable and, with that, the final acceptance of impotence. Like Ralph Marvell, his fellow-

representative of Old New York in *The Custom of the Country,*
Selden is "a survival, and destined, as such, to go down in any
conflict with the rising forces."[4] In William Faulkner's *The
Hamlet,* a similar form of stubborn complacency paralyzes an
entire community.

Thus, as Lily makes her final "descent" from Bellomont to her
last night in a dingy boarding house, she chooses to spurn
Selden's token efforts to rescue her and clings, instead, to her
idea (although she refuses, at the same time, to apply it for her
own benefit) that "the only way not to think about money is to
have a great deal of it" (p. 110)—that those who have less money
than the Trenors, for example, are actually more materialistic.
And in time, Lily does discover at least that the farther one sinks
below the upper crust of society, the greater are the numbers of
new aspirants, the more intense their ambition, and the more
hurried and resonant their quest for attention. Edith Wharton
very appropriately describes Lily's reaction to her first weekend
with the Gormers as an "odd sense of having been caught up
into the crowd as carelessly as a passenger is gathered in by an
express train" with its "deafening rattle and roar" (pp. 375, 376).
This image, significantly, is the same one that dominates the
novel's opening scene in Grand Central Station, the difference
being that, there, Lily is moving between "one and another of
the country-houses which disputed her presence" at a distinctly
slower pace and as much out of opportunity as necessity (p. 3).
Nevertheless, even at the outset of *The House of Mirth* the seeds of
Lily's imprisonment are inherent in her situation: the "gilt cage"
only seems less confining; and either train image suggests the
"great social machine" that plays havoc with Lily's dreams of
happiness and security. In book two of the novel, as the momentum of Lily's descent increases, each "house" she encounters is
like a further stop on the express train's accelerating journey;
she is excluded from society at one station and must rush to
board it at the next, all the time aware that the train is taking her
away from the destination she seeks. Her ultimate point of de-
barkation seems, quite literally, to be the end of the line.

But why does Lily continue to reboard the train, as it were, and yet each time manage to exclude herself from it? In part, the answer lies in her inveterate need to make irrelevant distinctions between the various "houses" she enters. She repeatedly makes too much of the differences between those who are inside and those who are outside what she calls "society," between the wealthy and mannered and the not-so-wealthy and unmannered. For all intents and purposes, the society that has entrapped her is, from top to bottom, the same; it shows itself at every point the handmaiden of history: amoral and capricious. Aside from her feelings and conduct toward Selden, the only valid moral distinction that Lily makes is her appreciation of Rosedale's honesty, which is a slight distinction indeed. Nevertheless, although confronted with a unanimity of amorality, Lily still feels obliged to make distinctions of some sort or other, and the only ones she can make are those of what Louis Auchincloss calls *scent*[5]—that is, according to the form of one's life, as opposed to its content or ethical value. In essence, for example, there is little difference between the Gormer milieu and Bellomont: the former has "more noise, more colour, more champagne, more familiarity," but it also has "greater good nature, less rivalry, and a fresher capacity for enjoyment" (p. 376). To the reader, these characteristics, in any moral sense, might seem to offset each other and make any significant distinction between the two societies seem immaterial. But Lily must make a judgment. The "hundred shades of aspect and manner, from the pattern of the men's waistcoats to the inflexion of the women's voices," which separate the Gormers's world from the fondly remembered house of mirth, convince Lily that the one is "only a flamboyant copy" of what she considers "her own world," her rightful place—a "caricature," it seems to her, "approximating the real thing as the 'society play' approaches the manners of the drawing-room" (p. 376).

The distinction is there, to be sure: the Gormers are trying to copy the Trenors and Dorsets in their own promiscuous way. Lily's error, rather, is in overestimating the significance of the distinction, in identifying herself (Selden would say unworthily) with the house of mirth. Likewise, after Lily aligns herself with

Mrs. Hatch in "the fashionable world of the New York hotel" (following her sojourn with the Gormers), she grows increasingly sensitive to the offenses of her employer, which "were always against taste rather than conduct" (p. 446). In the millinery shop, she is offended by the constant "current of meaningless sound" filled with "the mixture of insatiable curiosity and contemptuous freedom with which *she and her kind* were discussed in this underworld of toilers who lived on their vanity and self-indulgence" (p. 461; italics added). Once work has finished and Lily has departed from the throng of working girls, the author says "she always felt an irresistible return to her old standpoint, an instinctive shrinking from all that was unpolished and promiscuous" (p. 463). Why is Lily so unable to take the expedient course and adjust to her changing environment once her sources of money have been shut off and she has been excluded from the house of mirth? Why does she insist, in other words, on making the kinds of fastidious distinctions that can only hasten her journey toward poverty and despair?

In the first place, it is fair to say that for her to give in to expediency would violate her own sense of what is "appropriate" for herself. She needs to feel superior to each new environment, not at home in it. At the Gormers, for instance, Lily is most annoyed by the "hard glaze of indifference" that seems to be "fast forming over her delicacies and susceptibilities" (p. 378). Losing those "delicacies and susceptibilities" would mean, for Lily, losing her identity.

But Lily also needs the protection of a superior *community* to dispel her loneliness and welcome her into its aristocratic fold. Of course, such a community is nowhere to be found amongst the nouveaux riches and the nouveaux-nouveaux riches of New York City. The nearest available approximation of it for Lily is the Trenors's house of mirth, although she knows that the "mere display" of life at Bellomont cannot satisfy her "affinity to all the subtler manifestations of wealth" (p. 62). Nevertheless, she must continue, nostalgically, to make distinctions between the house of mirth and the other "houses" she encounters because not to do so would be an admission on her part that the Trenors's society is in truth no different from the Gormers's. She can not bear the possibility that she is adjusting, for example, to the "easy promiscuity" of the Gormer milieu; yet, paradoxically, the more she feels herself, at the Gormers, drifting back to "her former manner of life" with the Trenors, the more her "longing to get back to her former surroundings [at Bellomont] hardened to a fixed idea" (p. 381). To attain that goal, however, "she would have to exact fresh concessions from her pride," to squelch any tendency to be "stuck-up," any desire "to mark a sense of differences and distinctions" (p. 377).

This is Lily's multihorned dilemma: she needs the feeling of being a part of a community of social and moral distinction that will, in turn, set off her own "jewel-like rareness." To sacrifice her "tastes" to expediency would be to compromise her dreams more than they had already been compromised by her willingness to be used by the status seekers around her. Yet to cling to those same "tastes" only increases her nostalgic sense of loss and hastens her away from the house of mirth that she hopes to reenter. In lieu of a true aristocracy, she would prefer the society of Bellomont that best upholds the facade of respect and solidarity. When she finds that she is growing to tolerate the Gormers after disdaining them under other circumstances, she is faced with the possibility that either she was wrong before and, so, has not lost anything because she never had anything better, or she was right before and has compromised her own standards of judgment. Obviously, neither alternative is a happy one for Lily. Will she disparage the house of mirth or herself? Will she accept the falsity of Bellomont and experience again its impersonal safety (by using Bertha Dorset's letters to Selden against her), or will she continue to think highly of Bellomont and thereby manage to exclude herself forever from its precincts? Of course, she chooses the latter—the only alternative that, behind all her dubious distinctions between the various factions and families she encounters, will permit her to retain her own powers of distinction and a sense of her own personal worth. It is this that she wants Selden to understand in their final meeting: "that she had saved herself whole from the seeming ruin of her life" (p. 497).

With no hope in the end of keeping both her spirit and her life intact, Lily's spirit wins out. Around her, "all the men and women she knew were like atoms whirling away from each other in some wild centrifugal dance." Everyone seems to be without a "centre of earthly pieties, of grave endearing traditions, to which [one's] heart could revert and from which it could draw strength for itself and tenderness for others." Least of all does Lily have a "slowly-accumulated past" that might have given her a sense of "mysterious links of kinship to all the mighty sum of human striving" (p. 516). But at least Lily realizes her loss; and this self-awareness makes her simply the truest victim of "the whirling surface of existence" in an increasingly affluent democracy. In such a society, to quote de Tocqueville, everyone "behaves after his own fashion" whether he wants to or not, "and there is always a certain incoherence in the manners of such times, because they are molded upon the feelings and notions of each individual rather than upon an ideal model proposed for general imitation."[6]

Knowing this at the end of the novel, Lily Bart has nothing left but the most unbearable of all sensations in a democratic society: "the emptiness of renunciation" (p. 518). Perhaps one could argue that Lily's situation, in reaching this point, is more sympathetic and less ironic that either Madeleine Lee's in *Democracy* or Olive Chancellor's in *The Bostonians,* since Lily does not have the inherited wealth to support even the illusion of "grave endearing traditions"; she is at once more adrift and less self-deceived about her situation than they. And her feelings of nostalgia are therefore more desperate than theirs. Still, Lily Bart is no less a social being than Madeleine Lee or Olive Chancellor. The irony of Lily's life and dreams remains the error of a changing society that precipitously equates wealth and social security, as poor Nettie Struther does in her innocent admiration for Lily: "Work girls aren't looked after the way you are, and they don't always know how to look after themselves" (p. 509). There is no one to look after Lily in her moment of greatest need, and she dies. In the next chapter and novel, at the same moment of "suicide," Professor St. Peter is saved for his life of "renunciation."

6

"Roving tribes"
and "brutal invaders":
Willa Cather's
The Professor's House

Along with such novels as Henry Adams's *Democracy* and Allen Tate's *The Fathers*, Willa Cather's novel *The Professor's House* ranks as one of the most unfairly disregarded books in American literature. Even when it has been given the attention it deserves, as, for example, in Edward and Lillian Bloom's *Willa Cather's Gift of Sympathy*, it is generally treated as congruent with the spirit and tone of the author's more popular pioneering novels. Of course, the character of Tom Outland and his story of the Southwest, which comprises the lengthly second section of *The Professor's House*, do evoke the same veneration for primitive simplicity and lost values that one feels in such novels as *O Pioneers!*, *My Ántonia*, and *Death Comes for the Archbishop*. But unlike these and many of Willa Cather's other works, the strength and importance of *The Professor's House* are chiefly attributable to the fact that it is essentially not concerned with the pastoral or frontier life—with life "on the bright edges of the world," as Miss Cather called it in *Death Comes for the Archbishop*.

Tom Outland's story—his adventures on the Blue Mesa in

New Mexico and the discovery of the ancient Indian civilization with his lost friend Rodney Blake—is secondary to the story of Godfrey St. Peter, respected historian of Spanish exploration in North America and middle-aged professor at a state university on the shores of Lake Michigan. The first and longest section of the novel introduces Outland to the reader as St. Peter's most memorable student (after Outland had come north from New Mexico and before his death in World War I); the second section, Outland's story, stands apart and is related, ostensibly, as it is remembered by St. Peter; and the final and shortest section returns again to St. Peter and his thwarted "suicide."

As personalities, Outland and St. Peter interact throughout the novel, particularly in the mind of the professor, who remains the central intelligence of the novel. However, by allowing Outland's story to stand alone as a separate section, Willa Cather distracts the reader from St. Peter's situation and personality. Technically, Tom Outland is not (or rather should not be) a character in the events of the novel; nearly everything the reader learns about him is filtered through the mind of St. Peter—a "spiritual aristocrat" with "democratic manners," in Alfred Kazin's phrase.[1] The Professor has been isolated by the events of World War I from the one person—Outland—who has given him the most meaning during his life as a teacher and scholar. In the early years of the twentieth century, St. Peter assuaged his natural romantic longings by writing his multivolumed history of the Spanish adventurers in North America. Then, "just when the morning brightness of the world was wearing off for him, along came Outland and brought him a kind of second youth."[2] As the novel opens, however, Outland is already dead, and St.Peter is growing less and less able to cope with the petty commercialism of his academic routine in Hamilton, particularly the envy and greed generated by the success of a revolutionary vacuum invented by Outland at the university. To offset these feelings, St. Peter clings to his memories of Outland and, in general, dwells increasingly in the past. To the extent that it is more than simply a nostalgic evocation of a lost civilization in the Southwest, *The Professor's House* is an account of the professor's attempts to escape the painful realities of the present and retrieve, in some way, the second youth that Outland had once brought him like a reincarnation of one of his own Spanish explorers.

Primarily then, Outland's character functions in the novel as an image for St. Peter of an earlier, more adventuresome self of his own. In the final section of the novel, when St. Peter shelters himself in the old house where he wrote his histories and refuses to move into the new house he has built for his wife, the memory of Outland gradually becomes an obsession for him and finally an illusion that nearly leads him to self-destruction. Before he can survive in the present, St. Peter must recognize that Outland, at least in his own memory if not in actual life, was what his son-in-law Scott calls "a glittering idea" (p. 111); and, as such, St. Peter must eventually be able to feel toward Outland as he intermittently feels toward his finished histories: "that I've put a great deal behind me, where I can't go back to it again" (p. 163). This is the note of resignation on which the last section ends, and it is clear, despite the romantic appeal of Outland's adventures in the second section of the novel, that Willa Cather wants the reader to admire Professor St. Peter's ability to reach this final stage of self-awareness. It seems almost remarkable, therefore, that none of Willa Cather's critics, even when they have dealt at length with *The Professor's House,* have fully appreciated the honesty of her treatment of history in this novel, however revolted she was by the materialistic spirit of twentieth-century America. No one, in other words, has sufficiently plumbed the sense of inevitable resignation in *The Professor's House* and the ironies, intentional or not, that arise from St. Peter's own nostalgic attitudes toward history and toward the person of Tom Outland.

To understand the nature of St. Peter's anxieties, one must go, as Leon Edel perceived a number of years ago, beyond the idea that they are mainly the result of his growing older (though Edel's own contention that St. Peter has "everything to live for" and chooses not to live "for reasons unexplained and unresolved" is simply invalid).[3] "It's not wholly a matter of the calendar," as St. Peter confesses to his wife Lillian, who rebukes him for acting older than his fifty-two years. For a long time, she says,

> you never seemed to grow at all older, though I did. Two
> years ago you were an impetuous young man. Now you save
> yourself in everything. You're naturally warm and affection-
> ate; all at once you begin shutting yourself away from
> everybody. . . . I can't see any change in your face, though I
> watch you so closely. It's in your mind, in your mood. Some-
> thing has come over you (pp. 162, 163).

St. Peter has lost more than his own youth, he has lost the spirit
that he often associates with youth—the ability to approach life
as an adventure. When that spirit is gone, the confining walls of
one's environment seem to close in, the bloomless side of life
predominates, and the past supersedes the present or future in
its appeal.

The more the ordinary, rather self-absorbed society of Hamilton appears to conspire against the ideals that St. Peter
cherishes, the more he retires to the narrow privacy of his old
house, and the more he dwells nostalgically on those indefinable
qualities that made the past for him better than the present. By
divorcing himself from the day to day happiness of those around
him—his wife's trip to Europe with their oldest daughter and
son-in-law, for example—St. Peter can simplify his life to the
point of substituting his dreams for reality:

> He could simply insist that he must work, and that he couldn't
> work away from his old study. There were some advantages
> about being a writer of histories. The desk was a shelter one
> could hide behind, it was a hole one could creep into (p. 161).

Surrounded by his old comforts (a kerosene lamp, pot-bellied
stove, and French wine), "he could get isolation, insulation from
the engaging drama of domestic life" (p. 26).

As St. Peter's life continues to narrow, his memories continue
to expand. Thus, when he and his wife go to the opera in
Chicago and see the *Mignon* with its "expression of youth," he
declares, at first, that "it's been a mistake, our having a family

and writing histories and getting middle-aged. We should have been picturesquely shipwrecked together when we were young" (p. 94). Yet, on further examination, St. Peter discovers that even his wife is absent from his most precious memory: "Indeed, nobody was in it but himself, and a weather-dried little sea captain from the Hautes-Pyrénées, half a dozen spry seamen, and a line of gleaming snow peaks, agonizingly high and sharp, along the southern coast of Spain" (p. 95). The reader learns later that this was the moment years before when St. Peter first conceived in his imagination his history of the Spanish explorers in North America. To begin again his labor of love, to repeat that entire vicarious adventure in the same way, is St. Peter's fondest wish.

St. Peter himself, however, has been "born too late to be a pioneer," as one critic has put it.[4] Not only is it impossible for him to reenact throughout his life his adventures as a historian, but also, those adventures are, by nature, different from those of the Spanish explorers themselves. The difference is likewise what distinguishes Tom Outland and St. Peter: one is a man of action who knew hardship and disappointment; the other is a man of thought who "had never learned to live without delight" (p. 282). One has experienced "the adventurous side of history," while the other has had to write about it. In a sense, Professor St. Peter is Outland's Boswell, no more, no less. Perhaps more than he would like to think, he is the person whose job it is to commemorate "fellows like Outland," who, unlike a domesticated historian, "don't carry much luggage, yet one of the things you know them by is their sumptuous generosity—and when they are gone, all you can say of them is that they departed leaving princely gifts" (p. 121). The natural function of St. Peter's mind is the very thing that Outland had feared when he refused to return to the Blue Mesa for his diary: the danger, that is, of "going backward" into the past, like a historian, and running the risk of corrupting his experience by trying to retain it—of "[losing] the whole," Outland says, "in the parts" (p. 252).

Put another way, St. Peter's mind—the writer's mind—thrives on the symbolic, on the larger significance or representativeness of historical events, while Outland was himself too close to history to enjoy the luxury of a reflective imagination. Appropriately, the scientific format of the diary Outland kept on the mesa stands in direct contrast to St. Peter's lengthy volumes of history. To St. Peter's way of thinking Outland's plain account

> was almost beautiful, because of the stupidities it avoided and the things it did not say. If words had cost money, Tom couldn't have used them more sparingly. The adjectives were purely descriptive, relating to form and colour, and were used to present the objects under consideration, not the young explorer's emotions (p. 262).

It is up to St. Peter to detect and express "the kindling imagination" and "excitement of the boy" behind the austerity of the diary. To discover the meanings that lie behind men and events, to risk the"stupidities" of interpretation, is both the nature of St. Peter's task as a historian and the essence of his personality. He can not appreciate Outland, for example, without seeing in his life a larger significance than it had for Outland himself:

> his strange coming, his strange story, his devotion, his early death and posthumous fame—it was all fantastic. Fantastic, too, that this tramp boy should amass a fortune for someone whose name he had never heard, for "an extravagant and wheeling stranger." The Professor often thought of that curiously bitter burst from the barytone in Brahms's Requiem, attending the words, *"He heapeth up riches and cannot tell who shall scatter them!"* The vehemence of this passage had seemed to him uncalled for until he read it by the light of the history of his own family (pp. 257–58)

It therefore seems almost fitting to St. Peter that Tom Outland died before his vacuum had brought him wealth and fame:

> St. Peter sometimes wondered what would have happened to him, once the trap of worldly success had been sprung on him. He couldn't see Tom building "Outland" [the home built by St. Peter's daughter—and Outland's fiancée—with the money from Outland's will], or becoming a public-spirited citizen of

Hamilton. What change would have come in his blue eye, in his fine long hand with the backspringing thumb, which had never handled things that were not the symbols of ideas? A hand like that, had he lived, must have been put to other uses. His fellow scientists, his wife, the town and State, would have required many duties of it. It would have had to write thousands of useless letters, frame thousands of false excuses. It would have had to "manage" a great deal of money, to be the instrument of a woman who would grow always more exacting. He had escaped all that. He had made something new in the world—and the rewards, the meaningless conventional gestures, he had left to others (pp. 260–61).

The preceding passage has been quoted at length because of the insights it affords into St. Peter's personality rather than Outland's. The professor's fears for Outland are his own fears; the duties he speaks of are his own duties. Though St. Peter himself has not been able to escape the "meaningless conventional gestures" of day-to-day existence, he must believe that someone he once had the privilege of knowing did escape them. The fact that Outland was killed before he could be trapped by success only gives St. Peter's image of his "impersonality" an added sense of appropriateness and perfection. In a world in which everyone around him appears to be corrupted by compromises, St. Peter might have said, with the narrator of Sherwood Anderson's "Death in the Woods," that in Outland "a thing so complete has its own beauty."[5] To "see it as a whole," to "possess" the memory of Outland as Outland "saw" and "possessed" the Blue Mesa on his last night there, is St. Peter's desire. Then he could say, with Outland, that "something had happened in me that made it possible for me to coordinate and simplify, and that process, going on in my mind, brought with it great happienss" (pp. 250–51). St. Peter would like thus to "coordinate and simplify" the entirety of his own life through the memory of Tom Outland's personality and experience. For a "spiritual aristocrat" adrift in a democratic society, with "no other ancestors to inherit from" (p. 242), the idea of receiving in trust, through Outland, the lost secrets of a superior civilization has an irresistible appeal. It is, in Outland's words, like "the feeling of being . . . in a world above the world" (p. 240).

Indeed, the Indians' orderly and secure life in the Cliff City was "above" the rest of the world in virtue as well as height. As Father Duchene described it to Outland,

> they lived for something more than food and shelter. They had an appreciation of comfort, and went even further than that. . . . There is unquestionably a distinct feeling for design in what you call the Cliff City. . . . The workmanship on both the wood and stone of the dwellings is good. . . . I see your tribe . . . isolated, cut off from other tribes, working out their destiny, making their mesa more and more worthy to be a home for man (pp. 219, 220).

Feeling likewise isolated in the twentieth century, St. Peter shares with the lost tribe the "yearning for order and security" (p. 221). If he had his way, his life would also reflect an emphasis on convenience and comfort, but would ultimately, in the proportion and beauty of its design, have as its goal "something more than food and shelter." For St. Peter, as well as the Indian tribe, art and religion are inseparable: the aristocratic spirit dictates an essentially aesthetic way of life. "What makes men happy," the professor insists to his class, is

> believing in the mystery and importance of their own little individual lives. It makes us happy to surround our creature needs and bodily instincts with as much pomp and circumstance as possible. Art and religion (they are the same thing, in the end, of course) have given man the only happiness he has ever had (pp. 68–69).

Isolated atop the mesa, with their amphitheater for religion and sports and the observatory for watching the sky, the Indians are like St. Peter's men and women during the Renaissance who "crowded into the cathedrals on Easter Sunday" and were the principals "in a gorgeous drama with God, glittering angels on one side and the shadows of evil coming and going on the other. . . . The king and the beggar had the same chance at miracles and great temptations and revelations" (p. 68). That way of life, by St. Peter's standards, "was a rich thing."

But, put next to the inspiration of older, more stable, essentially aesthetic cultures, the politics and acquisitiveness of twentieth-century Washington and Hamilton seem a "slavish" and "petty" existence to Outland and St. Peter. The sight of "hundreds of little black-coated men pouring out of white buildings" in Washington (p. 236) depresses Outland much more than the image of workmen pouring out of a factory; at least the workers, like the Indians on the mesa, are making a "harder start" in life and are that much closer to the "sacred" goal of lifting themselves out of "mere brutality." If order and security characterize the Cliff City society, then disorder and insecurity are the natural state of affairs for the thousands of government clerks competing for influence and prestige; they all seemed to Outland "like people in slavery, who ought to be free" (p. 234). Everyone in Washington spends his life "trying to keep up appearances" (p. 232); even the scholarly secretary for the Director of the Smithsonian Institute, to Outland's amazement and disgust, found it "worth his while to show off before a boy, and a boy of such humble pretentions, who didn't know how to eat the hors d' oeuvres any more than if an assortment of cocoanuts had been set before him with no hammer" (p. 231).

St. Peter, for his part, discovers that a scholar in Hamilton is no less immune to the departmental life of politics and influence. The "new commercialism"—the "aim to 'show results' "—was "undermining and vulgarizing education" in the university.

> The State Legislature and the board of regents seemed determined to make a trade school of the university. Candidates for the degree of Bachelor of Arts were allowed credits for commercial studies: courses in bookkeeping, experimental farming, domestic science, dressmaking, and what not. Every year the regents tried to diminish the number of credits required in science and the humanities (p. 140).

The outcome of all this, from St. Peter's point of view, was a decline in the quality of the student body. Even Professor Crane, who fought for years in a common cause with St. Peter against the new commercialism, shows signs of sacrificing his former disinterestedness for the sake of wealth and power. As Outland's mentor in physics, Crane was once satisfied with the pursuit of knowledge. But when the proceeds of Outland's invention go to Rosamond and by her marriage to an "outsider" like Louie Marsellus, the disparity between their wealth and his poverty begins to sow in Crane the seeds of envy. In effect, Crane is sacrificing whatever moral advantage he might have had over those who had converted Outland's bones "into a personal asset" (p. 47). "Too much," St. Peter thinks, in reference to the money that was "corrupting" the lives of those around him, "is certainly worse than too little—of anything" (p. 154).

On this score, St. Peter's daughter Rosamond is the chief offender. Nearly every wife in *The Professor's House* is more ambitious than her husband. Marsellus himself belongs to that group of "new" characters in the American novel (along with men like Senator Ratcliffe in Adams's *Democracy* and Simon Rosedale in Edith Wharton's *The House of Mirth*) whose heedless enthusiasm and gregarious familarity clash, at times, with the more aristocratic temperaments of characters like Madeleine Lee, Lily Bart, and Godfrey St. Peter; nevertheless, the persistent vitality of Marsellus and his counterparts often gives them an engaging air of power and honesty. Perhaps this is because they frequently see and appreciate the best qualities in others; Louie, after all, is St. Peter's greatest admirer, despite their different styles of life. Though Marsellus's advent on the Hamilton scene is the primary cause of the selfishness and envy that seem, to St. Peter, to be dividing his family, it is also apparent that Louie alone has somehow managed to maintain his integrity:

> Since Rosamond's marriage to Marsellus, both she and her mother had changed bewilderingly in some respects— changed and hardened. But Louie, who had done the damage, had not damaged himself. It was to him that one appealed,—for Augusta, for Professor Crane, for the bruised feelings of people less fortunate (p. 161).

Louie's worldliness appears to be natural and consistent with his history and personality. In Lillian and Rosamond, however, the same worldliness—the "willingness to get the most out of occasions and people" (p. 160)—seems "unnatural" to St. Peter, a product, perhaps, of the unaccustomed affluence that precipitated them into "the little anxious social world of Hamilton" (p. 79). In a "world full of blunderers," as St. Peter puts it, his wife and daughter tend to make others "pay scrupulously for [their] mistakes" (p. 130). It seems a disgrace to St. Peter, for example, that Rosamond would refuse to help reimburse the family's housekeeper, Augusta, for a foolish stock-market purchase, just to teach her a lesson. And Lillian, in her own right, shows an equally harsh judgment of others' inferiority when she rebukes St. Peter for "cheapening" himself by talking to his students "as if they were intelligent beings" (p. 70).

Though he is no less conscious than his wife of the natural differences between people, St. Peter's whole approach toward others is based upon the eager encouragement of superiority, rather than the self-righteous discouragement of inferiority. His fondest memories, as has already been indicated, are of certain "fantastic" moments of distinction; and, precisely because they are so rare, they take on an added mythical distinction for the professor. Perhaps St. Peter could not have prevented Marsellus from capitalizing on Outland's invention and eventually becoming a member of the family, but the fact remains that St. Peter preferred to ignore the practical consequences of Outland's efforts. Even though, as he tells his younger daughter, he "wasn't in the mood to struggle with manufacturers," it is clear, from St. Peter's low opinion of science "as a phase of human development," that his memory of Outland would be sullied by its association with the "ingenious toys" of social progress. For St. Peter, those first years in Hamilton, "before Outland had done anything remarkable, were really the best of all" (p. 125). The private recollection of those times—"all those years when [Outland] was in and out of the house like an older brother" for his daughters, like his own son (p. 132)—is St. Peter's own personal possession. So it upsets him to hear Rosamond talk as if he should be reimbursed for all he did for Outland:

> Nothing hurts me so much as to have any member of my family talk as if we had done something fine for that young man, brought him out, produced him. . . . And there can be no question of money between me and Tom Outland. I can't explain just how I feel about it, but it would somehow damage my recollections of him, would make that episode in my life commonplace like everything else. And that would be a great loss to me. . . . My friendship with Outland is the one thing I will not have translated into the vulgar tongue (p. 62).

St. Peter must believe that Outland was one of those "miracles" that are revealed to king and beggar alike; it gives his own life a spiritual distinction totally divorced from the commonplace differences of wealth and influence.

With this in mind, it becomes clear that St. Peter's decision not to go to France with his family, because Paris is "too full of memories," is merely an excuse for plunging deeper into other, more important memories. To live alone again, with Outland's spirit for company, is to be, like the Indians on the Blue Mesa, "isolated, cut off from other tribes, working out [one's] destiny." Of course, the further one reads in book three of *The Professor's House,* the more one realizes that the eventual "destiny" of the Indian tribe—their extinction at the hands of an alien horde—is also the destiny that St. Peter imagines, and gradually desires, for himself. He is drawn to the "long, rugged, untamed vistas" of the Southwest, where he can merge with the "immortal repose" of lost civilizations. To this end, St. Peter conceives a more "primitive," aboriginal, and unmodified self—"the boy Godfrey" (not the other boy who cried when Lake Michigan disappeared over the horizon and "nearly died of" the wheat fields in central Kansas, or the young St. Peter who went to France, married, and became a respected scholar). Alone in his third-floor study or in his formal eighteenth-century garden, it seems to St. Peter that all those years, except for his brief boyhood in Kansas,

> had been accidental and ordered from the outside. His career, his wife, his family, were not his life at all, but a chain of events

which had happened to him. All those things had nothing to do with the person he was in the beginning (p. 264).

Since those early years, his life had been but

> a catching at handholds. One thing led to another and one development brought on another, and the design of his life had been the work of this secondary social man, the lover. . . . His histories, he was convinced, had no more to do with his original ego than his daughters had; they were a result of the high pressure of young manhood. . . . He seemed to know, among other things, that he was solitary and must always be so; he had never married, never been a father. He was earth, and would return to earth (pp. 264–65).

By dividing his "self," St. Peter has, in short, opted out of the problems and worries of his actual life. It is not simply a matter of being, or wanting to be, solitary; St. Peter had always guarded his privacy. Rather, it is, in essence, a longing for *extinction:* "now he thought of eternal solitude with gratefulness; as a release from every obligation, from every form of effort" (p. 272).

To want to be alone in great misfortunes is, as St. Peter tells himself, only natural; and the greatest misfortune is the "falling out of love." But for a person like St. Peter who (in his "second love affair" of the imagination) had always placed the highest value on an ideal society of order and security—an entire community of distinction—the loss of his ability to resist the commonplace and vulgar makes falling out of love seem like something doubly serious: a "falling out of all domestic and social relations, out of his place in the human family, indeed" (p. 275). As happier days retreat farther and farther into the past, one's dreams of the past and one's present existence become increasingly polarized. The battle is waged, not between two ways of life, but between life and death.

This is the final contest that engages St. Peter in the quiet of his old house while his family is in Paris. He can not by his own efforts, however, escape the dreams that threaten his future existence. Only after the wind in the sewingroom blows the stove out and the window shut (as his wife had always warned), does

St. Peter discover that death would indeed have been the victor had it not been for Augusta's fortuitous arrival on the scene. But he also discovers that all his meditations on the Truth of his original self were misguided; the true, instinctive Godfrey St. Peter was the one that clung to life in the sewingroom and tried to crawl to safety. Those who have been blessed with a miracle can not keep it all to themselves—that would be a betrayal of trust; they always need the helping hand of those who seem to be less fortunate. The fantastic side of life can not exist without the bloomless side to give it distinction; neither has, by itself, any staying power. Whatever is past is forever past, but there is, St. Peter thinks, still "a world full of Augustas, with whom one was outward bound" (p. 281).

The whole, as Outland said, can be lost in the parts, and St. Peter very nearly lost the whole of his life in his nostalgic memories of Outland. His mistake had been "in an attitude of mind," in the belief that nothing of value need ever be lost in life, that, regardless of the change in one's fortunes, one's spirit could, and should, remain immutable. But everything does change, and something is always lost. In a society where "brutal invaders" and "roving . . . tribe[s] without culture or domestic virtues" (p. 221) are the rule, rather than the exception, one must continually relinquish one's dreams of the past for the reality of the present even if those dreams are "something very precious." Then, in resignation, one can at least, like Professor St. Peter, begin to feel "the ground under his feet" (p. 283). "When you admitted that a thing was real," St. Peter concludes, "that was enough—now" (p. 281).

Willa Cather was, finally, less a romantic than a realist in *The Professor's House;* there, she saw the dangers as well as the attractions of nostalgia, in contrast to a novel like *My Ántonia,* where her own dominant nostalgia verges on a serious deprecation of herself as an artist (through the sad self-effacement of her narrator, Jim Burden). In *The Professor's House,* Willa Cather's subject was life on the bright edges of the mind *within* the world, not the bright edges of the world itself.

7

"The diminished grandeur of Washington Street": Ellen Glasgow's *The Sheltered Life*

If *The Sheltered Life* is Ellen Glasgow's best novel (as many critics have argued),[1] it is also her most distinctive. She herself likened it to *The Romantic Comedians* and *They Stooped to Folly* in its concern with "the place and tragicomedy of the individual in an established society." Together, these novels illustrate, she said, "the struggle of personality against tradition and social background."[2] This, in fact, is true of nearly every Glasgow novel, but in *The Sheltered Life,* despite the author's claim, the resistance of personality to tradition and social background is minimal. The struggle in this novel is not between the individual and his society, but between that society and history. The world of the Archbalds and Birdsongs is no longer "established" (except in their own "sheltered" illusions), but is instead, as Ellen Glasgow said elsewhere, "a slowly disintegrating world of tradition."[3] "The age was drifting." General Archbald thinks to himself at one point, "the world was flattening around him; the heroic mold had been broken. Beauty, like passion, would decline to the level of mediocrity. With the lost sense of glory, the power of personality would change and decay."[4]

To be sure, the decline of a romantic Southern society was frequently the subject of Ellen Glasgow's fiction. As Alfred Kazin has pointed out, "the great quality of the life she saw all about her was a simple and astonishing refusal to admit reality"[5]; and irony was the best means of exposing this fantasy world. Usually, however, Ellen Glasgow's ironies were modified either by a comic point of view that focused on the private illusions of individuals in a self-contained society (*The Romantic Comedians, They Stooped to Folly*), or by a moral earnestness that stressed the importance of individual fortitude in the struggle against social circumstance (*Barren Ground, Vein of Iron, In This Our Life*). In *The Sheltered Life,* on the other hand, Ellen Glasgow broadened the object of her ironies to include the illusions of an entire society whose resistance to the circumstances of social change is both useless and self-destructive.

Specifically, the drama of the novel centers on two "old country families"—the Archbalds and the Birdsongs—who are defending their oasis of "civilization" against the incursion of technological progress in the first decade of the twentieth century. In their old homes they look out "over the diminished grandeur of Washington Street to the recent industrial conquest of Queenborough" (Ellen Glasgow's fictitious Virginia city) and inhale, every so often, "a breath of decay, from the new chemical factory near the river," a whiff strong enough "to spoil the delicate flavour of living" (pp. 4, 5–6). Once there had been ten other families who had moved, after the Civil War, from their old plantations in the country into the city. Even when they had moved, the families had remained "knit together by ties of kinship and tradition, in the Sabbath peace that comes only to those who have been vanquished in war" (p. 6). "Here," Ellen Glasgow says eulogistically,

> they resisted change and adversity and progress; and here at last they were scattered by nothing more tangible than a stench. Those who could afford a fashionable neighbourhood fled in the direction of Granite Boulevard. Others retired to modest Virginian farms. Only the Archbalds and the Birdsongs, at the other end of the block, stood their ground and

watched the invasion of ugliness. The Birdsongs stayed because, as they confessed proudly, they were too poor to move;
and the Archbalds stayed because the General, in his seventy-
sixth year but still incapable of retreat, declared that he would
never forsake Mrs. Birdsong. Industrialism might conquer,
but they would never surrender (p. 6).

This passage alone indicates that Ellen Glasgow's criticism of
Southern romanticism, even in *The Sheltered Life,* is qualified.
There was something about the "heroic mold" of preindustrial
Virginia that she, too, recalled with the fondest nostalgia. "Un-
daunted," she says, "the two families held the breach between
the old and the new order, sustained by pride and by some
moral quality more enduring than pride" (p. 7). And, indeed, to
a great extent, *The Sheltered Life* is Ellen Glasgow's attempt to
dignify the "old elegance" and "personality" of Washington
Street in its battle against the impersonality of its changing environment. She felt that, in Kazin's words, "its addiction to illusion
was not something to be destroyed; it was one of those qualities
on which a culture is grounded, and without which it perishes."[6]
Nevertheless, it is only in *The Sheltered Life* that Ellen Glasgow
faced squarely the possibility that even such a society as this
could perish: "In Washington Street, where elegance had once
flourished and fallen, only the disfigured elms still struggled to
preserve the delusion of grandeur. . . . But it was useless to regret. It was useless to sigh for the plumed hearse of one's ancestors" (p. 173). No matter how selfish and "mediocre" or noisy
and smelly the present may seem, one can not escape it by retreating into "the smiling region of phantasy" with its "vague
brightness of memory" (pp. 24, 73), as Cora Archbald and Eva
Birdsong, in their separate ways, attempt to do. It becomes
dramatically clear in fact, as the novel progresses, that the world
of the Archbalds is being destroyed as much by its own indige-
nous weaknesses as by any outside forces. To get or keep what one
wants, General Archbald discovers, "courage alone . . . was not
sufficient. For courage, as well as cowardice, may trust in false
values—even in evasive idealism" (p. 101). Industrialism and
social change will indeed conquer its resistors ("swallow us

whole," George Birdsong says), and it will happen that much sooner because of the romantic escapism that characterizes the families' refusal to face the inevitability of the eventual "surrender" that concludes the novel.

In particular, the Archbalds and Birdsongs attempt to defend themselves against the passage of time by dwelling on youth—in the person of Jenny Blair Archbald, the novel's sheltered adolescent—and on the past—in their nostalgic memories. "The Age of Make-Believe" (the first section of the novel) could easily refer to either. Perhaps by keeping "the surface of life smooth and agreeable" (p. 368) and thereby protecting her daughter from the truth when it hurts, Mrs. Archbald (the General's daughter) is demonstrating what Ellen Glasgow calls "that last amenity of civilization, the power to control emotion" (p. 304). Cora's "persevering hypocrisy" does receive the author's commendation in the following description, for example: "a living triumph of self-discipline, of inward poise, of the confirmed habit of not wanting to be herself, she had found her reward in that quiet command over circumstances" (p. 243). Still, in raising Jenny Blair to be what Louis Auchincloss has called "a debutante of the ante-bellum era,"[7] Mrs. Archbald's "realm of phantasy" becomes "a small, enclosed province, peopled by skeletons of tradition and governed by a wooden theology" (p. 98). Appearances supersede reality. When Aunt Isabella Archbald falls in love with a carpenter, Joseph Crocker, her sister must find a suitable family tree for her future brother-in-law; Aunt Etta's neurasthenia and self-pity must be appeased not rebuked; and, in the case of Queenborough's legendary beauty, Eva Birdsong, the appearance of happiness, despite her husband's infidelity, is maintained and admired simply because it is known to be an appearance. Mrs. Archbald sees beneath Eva's "vision of serene elegance" but insists approvingly that even if her neighbor "knew everything" she "would never betray herself." "When happiness failed her," Cora says, "she would begin to live on her pride, which wears better. Keeping up an appearance is more than a habit with Eva. It is a second nature" (p. 25).

The unfaithful and masochistic George Birdsong thus becomes the villain of Washington Street because he has "no pride" when Eva, for instance, has her hysterectomy; "nobody ought to look stripped to the soul," General Archbald thinks, referring to George. "Surely there was nothing worse in a crisis than the way it tore away all pretenses" (pp. 248, 246). It is not, however, George's indiscretions themselves but rather his desperate need to keep up appearances, to keep those indiscretions a secret, that leads, by twists and turns, to his own death at the end of the novel. The need for pretenses creates more and greater crises. George must swear Jenny Blair to secrecy when she finds him at his mistress's home; but the secret then becomes an adventure for Jenny Blair until, eight years later, George's indulgence of her infatuation for him and his failure to treat her as anything but a little girl eventually precipitate his wife's act of revenge. The importance of keeping up appearances leads to "harmless" violations, which make appearances in the future even more inviolable. But Jenny Blair thinks this is the normal romance of life; after her original agreement with George, for example, she believes that henceforth "she would have a part in that mysterious world where grownup persons hide the things they do not wish children to know" (p. 68). Consequently, when she finally must face the unreality of her infatuation (which George has helped to encourage), "her whole being seem[s] to recoil from the hard surface of facts, and to fold, depth on depth, into the happier world of her memory" (p. 359). Her situation, like her sick Aunt's, becomes a metaphor for the self-deception and self-destruction of their society; in either case, the more tenderly they are treated, and the more their "poor health," or romantic illusions, dominate the Archbald household, the more obstinate the family's malady becomes.

That malady (as self-perpetuating and literally fatal as it finally is) is the combination of deception and grace that John Welch, the most modern character in the novel, calls "not facing things, trying to pretend that anything you don't wish to look at doesn't exist. It's a false attitude, of course, even if it is a noble one" (p. 370). Whether it is, in fact, a noble attitude is left in doubt by Ellen Glasgow's novel, but it is certainly a false attitude, and its falsity lies ultimately in the class consciousness that the Archbalds and Birdsongs will not surrender in the face of a changing world. The only hope for Washington Street's "delusion of grandeur" may be, as the General thinks, Joseph Crocker's infusion of some plebian blood into the family:

> After all, class consciousness, like his arteries, was not all that it used to be. Like every other superstition, he supposed, it was doomed to decay. Perhaps new blood, new passions, and new social taboos were the only salvation of a dying order (p. 102).

Yet, within *The Sheltered Life,* nothing can come of that possibility until the foreboding atmosphere that permeates the novel (the Birdsong's frog "prophetically" croaks "of the evil to come") is dispelled by the final violent catharsis of an entire society.

Old General Archbald is the wisest character in *The Sheltered Life,* but there is clearly nothing he can do to alter the events occurring around him. On the one hand, he is a "misfit," a man "born out of his time" who doesn't quite accept the conventional beliefs of his society (p. 31). On the other hand, he often seems merely the feeble embodiment of a recalcitrant, romantic age. He thinks that "there was wisdom in an era that smothered truth in words. For truth, in spite of the stern probings of science, is an ugly and terrible thing" (p. 131). Though the present was "softer" than the past for the General,

> he couldn't see that it was an improvement—except in the way one could turn on a bath or a light, or warm one's self through and through instead of merely toasting one's front or back by a fire. . . . A world made, or even made over, by science was only a stark and colourless spectacle to old David Archbald. . . . His eyes were old eyes, not to be trusted. They still looked at life through the iridescent film of a more romantic age. (pp. 174–75, 145, 186).

Thus, from his point of view, the material changes he witnesses in the twentieth century—from its inferior architecture to its noisy automobiles—seem "pathetic": "Even the sounds of the present, and certainly the smells, were less romantic than they used to be" (p. 179).

Ellen Glasgow once wrote that "The Deep Past" (General Archbald's long reverie and the central section of the novel) was "the whole book in a crystal."[8] "In General Archbald, the real protagonist," as she said elsewhere, "I was dealing with the fate of the civilized mind in a world where even the civilizations we make are uncivilized."[9] The problem with this kind of assistance from the author, however, is that it raises more questions than it answers. If General Archbald is the most civilized character in the novel, for example, is it not also true that he is the most powerless? Moreover, are not the greatest crises in *The Sheltered Life* the result of too much civilization—that is, too much refinement and pretense—rather than too little? And in dwelling privately on the "defeated passion" of his own youth (sacrificed, he realizes, to a lifetime of pretenses), is not the General nostalgically escaping the present as surely as the society that clings to its traditional pretenses? Both, in their own ways, manifest a "worship of adolescence." Whether in the form of his "astonishing sympathy with the revolt of youth" or in his determination, as he tells Jenny Blair, to "keep all knowledge of suffering out of your life" (pp. 173, 224), General Archbald is paying strict allegiance to the innocence that he and his society have already lost with the passage of time.

His whole life, in fact, has been a matter of "saving his own or some other person's appearance" (p. 32). He has "sacrificed his youth, his middle age, his dreams, his imagination, all the vital instincts that make a man, to the moral earnestness of tradition" (p. 33). Then, in his old age, "he had accepted the sense of something missing as a man accepts bodily disfigurement" (p. 163). At least this awareness of his loss sets him apart from the other characters in *The Sheltered Life* and gives him, in addition, a fleeting sense of the futility of even his nostalgia: "at eighty-three," he thinks, "it did no good to have a buried poet pop up from the depths and caper gallantly on the frozen surface of pretense" (p. 171). Nevertheless, there are certain treasured images of tradition that General Archbald will not relinquish under any circumstances, chief among which is his adoration of Eva Birdsong as the last of the "queenly women." Shortly before the novel's final violent episode, he dozes in his garden, "dreaming of Eva Birdsong, clinging, with the tenacity of age, to his last illusion. . . . It brought serenity of mood; it brought the courage of dying; it brought, even, acceptance of life. 'After all,' he found himself repeating aloud, 'character may survive failure. Fortitude may be the last thing to go' " (pp. 378, 379). Of course, the irony here is that, in the next scene, Eva's "fortitude" does "go," ultimately because too many people, like General Archbald, have idolized her and systematically widened the gulf over the years between her self-image and her husband's self-image. After Eva has killed George, General Archbald's last words to his screaming granddaughter are merely a pathetic instance of an entire society's confusion and self-deception:

> Turning away from Mrs. Birdsong, the old man spoke in a wandering tone, with an effort to separate his words as he uttered them. "Don't be brutal, John. The shock has unnerved her. Remember how young she is, and how innocent." Stretching out his old arms, he added gently, "It is too much for you, my darling. You had better go home and wait for your mother" (pp. 394–95).

Even murder can not penetrate the "frozen surface of pretense"—the habitual desire to shelter the innocent.

In continuing to put Mrs. Birdsong on a pedestal, though to the rest of Queenborough she is "one of those celebrated beauties, who, if they still exist, have ceased to be celebrated" (p. 19), the old families of Washington Street are hastening their own obsolescence and destruction. Their survival, as well as hers, depends, as far as they are concerned, upon the "heroic" aspects of life. She had fallen in love with George Birdsong when as a boy he calmly rescued Memoria, the family maid and his future mistress, from a fire in the slums of Queenborough. From then on, Eva insisted upon his lasting courage and, after their marriage, on the finality of his love. Thus her whole life became a "gallant endeavor to defend an illusion" (p. 200). "I staked all my happiness on a single chance," she tells Jenny Blair, "I gave up all the little joys for the sake of the one greatest joy" (p. 284). Originally, George, too, had fallen in love with her "because she was an ideal, and she [had] determined to remain his ideal until the end" (p. 271). But Eva's determination to believe in George's idealization of herself forces upon him an inflexible standard of conduct that merely accentuates his growing feelings of inferiority and guilt (over ending his wife's potential career as a concert soprano). In this effort, she has the unquestioned assistance of all the Archbalds, from Jenny Blair to the General; if she "expects too much of life," as one of her friends says (p. 118), they expect too much of her. In effect, her continued endurance becomes the test, for them, of their own values and traditions. Thus the General, like his daughter, tries to convince himself that Eva, "for all her loveliness," is "a strong soul in affliction" and incapable of self-pity (p. 136). Despite his sympathy for George's wayward passions ("his very faults were the too lavish defects of generosity"), he reserves his admiration for Eva's heroic adherence to their Southern "code of perfect behavior" (p. 193). Whether her concern for the appearance of happiness is in defiance of the truth about George or simply in ignorance of it is unimportant by these standards.

With "The Illusion" (the third and longest section of *The Sheltered Life*), however, Eva's defenses, and those of her society, begin to break down. The hysterectomy symbolizes for her the loss of the beauty that has been the measure of her reputation in Queenborough; since she well knows that George married her because she was an ideal for him, the operation awakens her fears of permanently losing his love and loyalty, of submitting *in vain* to the "exacting pretense" of her life (p. 245). The less her pride is rewarded by circumstances, the weaker it becomes. Consequently, when the General visits her in the hospital before the operation, he notices "all the faint lines traced by sorrow or anxiety about her eyes, and the deeper impression between her finely arched nose (the nose of a goddess, they had said in the 'nineties) and the rich curve of her mouth. Yes, she was yielding, however gallantly, to the slow deposit of time" (p. 186). But her surrender is more than physical: at home, after the operation, there is "the flicker of some deep hostility" in her eyes (p. 277)—a growing feeling of self-pity and anger. And later, when Jenny Blair returns from her summer vacation, Mrs. Birdsong breaks down in her presence, prompting the girl to swear to herself "that she would sooner die than hurt Mrs. Birdsong. To see her changed, stricken, defeated by life, with all her glory dragged in the dust, was too terrible. It was not that she had lost youth alone, but that she had lost everything" (p. 362). Moments before her final, long-repressed act of self-assertion, Eva tells Jenny Blair that "I'm worn out with being somebody else—with being somebody's ideal. I want to turn round and be myself for a little while before it is too late, before it is all over" (p. 386).

But it is already "too late." Unknown to either, Eva and Jenny Blair have been on a collision course throughout the novel, with George their waiting victim; both cling to their separate romantic illusions about the same man. In the case of Jenny Blair, Mrs. Archbald insists that her daughter's sympathies go beyond "the impenetrable egotism of youth": "she has a great deal of feeling. Only in some ways she takes after me, and the deeper her feeling, the less able she is to express it" (p. 231). But the General's intermittent doubts about Jenny Blair's "youthful" sympathies are more to the point. The habitual pretense of one generation has become, in her, the instinctive game of the next. If Jenny Blair does "not know the first thing about life," as her mother says toward the end of the novel (p. 325), it is because that is the way she has been raised—to believe that life is merely a game without the slightest tinge of tragedy. She is, in John Welch's words, "like every other young girl who has grown up without coming in touch with the world. You are so bottled up inside," he tells her, "that your imagination has turned into a hothouse for sensation" (p. 338).

Whatever is unknown and forbidden thus becomes romantic for Jenny Blair: as a nine year old, it is the curious smells coming from Penetentiary Bottom, and, with the initial secret between herself and George Birdsong, the hopeless passion she begins to feel for him becomes "far more romantic than the happy end of all the fiction she was permitted to read" (pp. 226–27). "All she wanted," she thinks, "was to love in vain and for ever, to feel this longing hidden safe away in her heart" (p. 317). She certainly "did not mean the slightest harm in the world" to anybody, especially Eva Birdsong; but she decides that "it can't harm her to have me love him in secret" (p. 279).

For his part, George Birdsong plays upon Jenny Blair's pity for his helplessness. When she meets him outside the hospital, before Eva's operation, he looks "harrassed and miserable." "Even his hard, strong body appeared to have given way and softened within from an invisible break" (p. 211). In his subsequent catalogue of ills and worries he becomes, in Jenny Blair's eyes, the manageable man:

> "I haven't had a wink of sleep for two nights and scarcely any for a week," Mr. Birdsong said, and his tone sounded hurt and astonished, as if he were protesting against an injustice. "How can I sleep when Eva is going through hell? I was afraid to drop off lest she should wake up and want me. And now my nerves are all shot to pieces. Don't get the idea I've been drinking. I haven't. I haven't touched a drop, and I'm not going to touch a drop until all this is over." . . . Never before had she seen him stripped of his charm, his gaiety, his effervescent good-humor. Yet, in some strange way she couldn't explain, she found that she liked him better when he appeared merely human and suffering (pp. 212–13).

In effect, Jenny Blair dissociates in her own mind the fallible man she "loves" from the perfect woman she "adores"—an assumption of inequality that reinforces George's own feelings of imperfection and inferiority. Though he only kisses her three times in the course of the novel, he sees the volatile effect it has on her. His solution, however, is to call her a troublemaker and then continue to treat her (at age seventeen or eighteen) as an innocent child. Like everyone else in the novel, George envies her youth and refuses to restrict it—"I adore youth, and you are—well, youth adorable" (p. 336).

Except for George's revelation of his own helplessness, Jenny Blair would prefer not to see beyond the pretense of her society.

"Trouble was a drab word," she thinks (p. 113). "No matter how hard she tried, she could not make herself feel that illness and death really touched her. . . . She adored Mrs. Birdsong . . . so passionately that it was impossible to associate her with illness or death" (p. 210). Thus, at the Peyton's party, when George slips away with Delia Barron and Eva goes into hysterics, Jenny Blair is seized by a "feeling of moral nakedness." "More than anything in the world," Ellen Glasgow says, "she hated to see her elders begin to crumble on the surface and let glimpses through of feelings that ought never to be expressed, not even in the direst extremity" (p. 122). What is forbidden must remain forbidden and unattainable for Jenny Blair, except, as she discovers, when her own passions are at stake. Then her question—"Hadn't she, when all was said, a right to a little happiness?" (p. 326)—becomes both a self-indulgent expression of youth and, as such, a valid condemnation of a society that insists upon her perennial innocence.

"Nothing in life is so precious as innocence," General Archbald concludes nostalgically (p. 236). True as that may be, however, Ellen Glasgow's novel demonstrates that innocence can be made destructive by the systematic attempt to preserve it. To their credit, both Eva and George Birdsong seem eventually to understand this fact, though they fail to apply its lesson fully to the danger of Jenny Blair. After he kisses her for the last time, for example, George momentarily grasps the significance of her age, his age, and perhaps the age of the "code" that condemns him yet gives him, at the same time, his negative identity: "Whether you know it or not," he scolds her, "innocence when it lives to be eighteen is wicked" (p. 354). Then, however, he dismisses her by saying naively, "We'll settle down and be chums again" (p. 356). Likewise, Eva, after the nervous breakdown that succeeds her operation, tells Jenny Blair that "I sometimes think that all the cruelty of youth—and nothing in the world is so cruel as youth—comes from not knowing what trouble is." But she, too, insists that "you are too young to know what trouble is" (p. 366).

Despite their awareness of the dangers of innocence, the Birdsongs are prime examples of the many characters in *The Sheltered Life* who confirm General Archbald's discovery that "not the young alone, but the old also, were seeking a false youth in recovered sensation" (p. 373). Whether in the form of the General's own nostalgic memories of the past—of the "poet" that might have been (like Professor St. Peter's "unmodified self"); in Eva Birdsong's determination to live by a code that idealized her youth and beauty; or in Cora's, George's, and Jenny Blair's adoration of Eva's "perfection," the last aristocratic residents of Washington Street resist the passage of time (with the physical and social changes it brings) and invite their own destruction. Ironically, in the character of Jenny Blair Archbald, the innocence that her society has sought most to protect as an ideal image of its own youth becomes, in the final confrontation between George, Eva, and herself, the agent of its destruction. The society of lower Washington Street, Queenborough, Virginia, has turned on itself and committed suicide.

To perceive the inevitable frustration of those who "live in dreams" and resist the course of history takes an ironic eye that is rare in American literature. Because Ellen Glasgow and some other American novelists have at times been able to dramatize "the breach between the old and the new order" as it has repeatedly appeared in the history of American society, their ironic vision has served to "shelter" them, in turn, from the persistent romantic failings of their characters.

8

"The shock of communion": Allen Tate's *The Fathers*

Both Allen Tate's *The Fathers* and A. B. Guthrie, Jr.'s *These Thousand Hills* (discussed in chapter ten) represent, in some sense, a departure from the kind of novel described in the preceding chapters. Essentially, the chief protagonist in each work—George Posey and Lat Evans—is identified with neither an old order nor a new order; he embodies social change while yearning and striving, at the same time, for social stability. Like Simon Rosedale in *The House of Mirth,* he has the personal ambition and, in time, the economic power that he hopes will qualify him for the society of his dreams. Rosedale succeeds because admission into the company of the Trenors and Dorsets does, in fact, depend upon his wealth; but George Posey and Lat Evans fail as long as their ambitions for order and stability represent a denial of their own material success and of the historical forces that are constantly altering the society that determines their fate. Though less nostalgic and more powerful than earlier victims of social change in American literature, such as Madeleine Lee and Godfrey St. Peter, they are no less self-deceived about their time and place in history, nor is the way of life they desire for themselves less "aristocratic" than that to which Mrs. Lee and Professor St. Peter had become accustomed. In the end, they are merely divided against themselves, rather than against any new "types" that might seem to threaten their security.

Certainly Arthur Mizener's description of the "central tension" in *The Fathers* could well apply to nearly every other novel thus far discussed in this study:

> We see, on the one hand, the static condition a society reaches when, by slow degrees, it has disciplined all personal feeling to custom so that the individual no longer exists apart from the ritual of society and the ritual of society expresses all the feelings the individual knows. We see, on the other hand, the forces that exist—because time does not stand still—both within and without the people who constitute a society, that will destroy the discipline of its civilization and leave the individual naked and alone.[1]

This is precisely the dramatic situation, for example, in *The Sheltered Life*—a "civilized" society that, too long, agrees "to let the abyss alone" and thereby invites the violence that leads to its own destruction.

In the events of *The Fathers,* which cover a period from 1858 to 1861—over forty years before the events of Ellen Glasgow's novel—the "ritual of society" is represented by the aristocratic Virginia family of Major Lewis Buchan, whose only daughter Susan marries George Posey. Although they had once been a "respectable family" with "considerable landed property and servants," the Poseys had moved from the country into Georgetown when George was a boy in the 1840s. There, unable to " merge into the small middle class of folks who were beginning to rise,"[2] the Poseys shut themselves up in a tall, red brick house and retired into separate rooms, the shells of their individual personalities. It was a world, in contrast to the "custom" of Buchan society, "where people communicated only through their infirmities, in hushed voices, a world in which the social acts became privacies" (p. 182). Caught somehow between the past, in the form of a stable social order, and the future, in the form of financial prosperity, George Posey "was a man without people or place; he had strong relationships, and he was capable of passionate feeling, but it was all personal" (p. 179). It is this "personal" aspect of George Posey's character that conflicts with the decorum of the Buchan family and eventually "destroys the discipline of its civilization." Susan grows to hate and fear the Poseys and seeks, at any cost, to prevent her brother Semmes's marriage to George's sister. And the cost, in the end, is tremendous, particularly for the Buchans: George kills Semmes, under the strangest of circumstances, and Susan goes insane.

Allen Tate's narrator, Lacy Buchan (Semmes and Susan's younger brother), has lived through this process of family disintegration and, fifty years later, as "an unmarried old man, having nothing else to do, with a competence saved from the practice of medicine" (p. 5), has decided to tell his story. "Is it not something to tell," he asks,

> when a score of people whom I knew and loved, people beyond whose lives I could imagine no other life, either out of violence in themselves or the times, or out of some misery or shame, scattered into the new life of the modern age where they cannot even find themselves? (p. 5).

But Lacy Buchan's function as the narrator of *The Fathers* is significant beyond the basic fact of his own involvement in the events he describes. It is important, first of all, that he grows up, perhaps because of, but at least simultaneously with, the disintegration of his family; this allows him, in his old age, to tell his story realistically and ironically—that is to say, with a degree of emotional and moral detachment. He has managed to escape the fate of people like his own relatives, "living in formal societies, lacking the historical imagination," who "can imagine for themselves only a timeless existence" without beginning or end (p. 183). Thus, Lacy is able years later to put the original indiscretions of George Posey—which had once been so dramatic in the past—into a larger, historical perspective. Neither oblivious to time and change, like his father, nor lost in time and change, like George, Lacy can comprehend and express, in his narrative, an existence that is far from timeless. When he recounts, for instance, his mother's funeral and his brother-in-law's refusal to participate, Lacy recalls that, as the family was about to depart for the graveyeard,

> the moment had come that all this waiting had been for, but it was lost in each new movement, each new step into our places in the melancholy procession. There was of course no one moment that it was all leading up to, and that piece of knowledge about life, learned that day, has permitted me to survive the disasters that overwhelmed other and better men, and to tell their story. Not even death was an instant; it too became a part of the ceaseless flow, instructing me to beware of fixing any hope, or some terrible lack of it, upon birth or death, or upon love or the giving in marriage. None of these could draw to itself all the life around it or even all the life in one person; not one of them but fell short of its occasion, warning us all to fear, not death, or love, or any ecstasy or calamity, but rather to fear our own expectancy of it, good or ill, or our own lack of preparation for these final things (p. 101).

If Lacy's age as a narrator thus gives him an appreciation of the inevitability of change and disappointment, his youth as a participant in the events of his story gives him an additional importance as the central consciousness of Tate's novel. His "savage sense of propriety so acute in children" (p. 14) makes him, to begin with, particularly attuned to the "extraordinary and violent," especially the "mystery and imagination" that the figure of George Posey evokes in nearly all the Buchan children (even though Susan and Semmes are both in their twenties). "A child," Lacy reflects, "expecting nothing of people, is shocked only when what happens has not happened before" (p. 14). It is not just the Civil War, but history itself that is irrepressible in *The Fathers,* and Lacy's youth gives him a proper sense, for Tate, of the alien and irresistible. His very love for an outsider like George Posey is an indication of the breakdown in the Buchan order, much as Jenny Blair's romantic attraction for the unknown and forbidden is a symptom, and finally a cause, of the self-destruction that concludes *The Sheltered Life.* "I admired George Posey," Lacy says, "even when I did not understand him, for I shared his impatience with the world as it was, as indeed every child must whose discipline is incomplete. He could do the things that I should lose the desire to do by the time I was grown and my own master" (p. 44).

As a child, "you remember what you cannot understand" (p. 272). Only later, in his old age, can Lacy as narrator begin to make sense of the violence he witnessed, but, by then, there is no point for him in "fixing blame." "I was so young, that when I knew everything it was too late to judge it, and there was too much to be said on both sides" (p. 132). A passionate barometer of change as a boy and a dispassionate recorder of change as a man, Lacy Buchan is a skillful vehicle for Allen Tate's own historical imagination.

The central conflict between George Posey and the propriety of the Buchan manner of life is described by Lacy early in the novel:

> Our lives were eternally balanced upon a pedestal below which lay an abyss that I could not name. Within that invisible tension my father [Major Buchan] knew the moves of an intricate game that he expected everybody else to play. That, I think, was because everything he was and felt was in the game itself; he had no life apart from it and he was baffled, as he had been baffled by George Posey, by the threat of some untamed force that did not recognize the rules of his game (pp. 43–44).

It is a game in which, for the rest of the Buchans as well as the Major, one's private self is inseparable from the public forms of one's daily life. Thus, Lacy, speaking as a Buchan, declares that it was impossible to distinguish the "domestic trials," growing out of his mother's death and George's conduct, from the "public crisis" of secession and the coming war:

> they worked together for a single evil, and I think *the evil was the more overwhelming among us because of the way men had of seeing themselves at that time:* as in all highly developed societies the line marking off the domestic from the public life was indistinct. Our domestic manners and satisfactions were as impersonal as the United States Navy, and the belief widely held today, that men may live apart from the political order,

that indeed the only humane and honorable satisfactions must be gained in spite of the public order, would have astonished most men of that time as a remote fantasy, impossible of realization (pp. 125–26; italics added).

In such a situation, when one's real self is one's social self, the slightest departure from the accustomed routine has, as in *The Fathers,* profound implications. And it is in this sense that ritual behavior, depending on its degree of inflexibility, can become self-defeating. As the momentum of events begins to accelerate toward the novel's violent climax, Lacy reflects, with the knowledge that has come with age, that "we are like children playing drop-the-handkerchief; the conventions make the emotions that we are willing to die for, as children eagerly run themselves to exhaustion round a ring" (p. 220).

In *The Fathers,* the "exhaustion" of the Buchan family begins when George Posey insists upon giving Lacy a rifle without first asking the Major's permission. Later, it seems to Lacy that there was nothing his bewildered father could do;

> his visitor hadn't been rude in any sense that papa knew rudeness; he had, as a matter of fact, been courteous. He had simply refused to recognize the only danger-signals that papa knew how to give, and he, George Posey, ought to have been the guardian of his own safety (p. 36).

As if this were not enough, however, George proceeds to press his advantage and calmly announces that he intends to marry Lacy's sister, Susan. To this, Major Buchan merely "tossed his head. Big man that he was, he was on his feet like an acrobat. He threw his head back and opened his mouth, but no words came. A look of innocent wonder spread over his face, the incredulity he might have felt on first contemplating a flying-machine" (p. 38).

This scene is followed, in turn, by George's inability to tolerate the ritual that surrounds the funeral of his mother-in-law, Mrs. Buchan. The Major, on the other hand, carries out his obligations to an impersonal code of conduct: "the old gentleman was crushed but in his sorrow he knew what everybody else was feeling, and in his high innocence he required that they know it too and be as polite as he" (p. 98). Here, of course, the Buchans' conventions are not affected to any great extent by George's offense. Though Lacy must eventually come to terms with his brother-in-law's conduct, his father "had no need to learn nor even to understand it, for to him there could have been nothing whatever to understand" (p. 101).

Only with the threat of war the following year does the impersonal Buchan routine begin to crack. A slight alteration one January day in the family's morning prayers (the Major's substitution of the phrase "notwithstanding our dangers" for a more general, more affirmative statement) is the first indication for Lacy. Then, with the bombardment of Fort Sumter in April, the family loyalties are split: Semmes and the other able-bodied men for the Confederacy, the Major still for the Union, and George Posey for neither. Since to be a Buchan was "to be possessed by only one idea at a time," the conflict between son and father is itself irrepressible and leads, eventually, to Semmes's disinheritance by his father, "whose politics," Lacy concludes in retrospect, "had closed his eyes and whose honor accepted the results of his politics and drove him to the formal repudiation of his son" (p. 254). Convinced that the trouble in South Carolina "don't affect us at all" and that "the madness will subside" (pp. 140, 151), the Major believes "that his neighbors alone [are] perversely opposing the Federal Government" (p. 176). He seems to Lacy like

a man preoccupied with some private mystery that could not be connected with what was going on in the world. How easy to think that "a show of force" would disband the Alexandria Rifles and Mt. Vernon Guards! Where in his mind were the vast hordes of young men who were rushing to village and county town, from the river bottoms and the hills, coming with squirrel rifles, shotguns, bowie knives, to "form military companies" in Georgia, Alabama, Mississippi, by the banks of the James, the Chattahoochee, the Tennessee? For papa, these young men did not exist; all that country from below the James to the Rio Grande was a map, and the "war" was about to be fought between the "government" and the sons of his neighbors and kin in the old Northern Neck of Virginia (p. 155).

Lacy remembers a remark his Cousin John Semmes once made to him about his father:

> Your pa is still living before he was born—in 1789. He thinks the government is a group of high-minded gentlemen who are trying to yield everything to one another. Damn it, Lacy, it's just men like your pa who are the glory of the Old Dominion, and the surest proof of her greatness, that are going to ruin us (p. 124).

But if it is difficult for Major Buchan to understand the fact of war and his son's commitment to the Confederacy, it is impossible for him to comprehend George Posey's complete lack of loyalties. Unlike the Buchans, George "could take both views of anything" (p. 250). Thus, instead of fighting openly for the South, he becomes a supplier and smuggler of its weapons, always remaining behind the scenes and insisting to Major Buchan that he does "prefer the Union." "I am not choosing sides," he says, "I am chosen by circumstances" (p. 149). As such, he distinguishes himself from those who indulge in the "nonsense" of fighting: "Mr. Semmes," he complains at one point, "your people are about to fight a war. They remind me of a passel of young 'uns playing prisoners' base" (pp. 166–67). Cousin John tries to convince Lacy that George is indeed one of "our people," but Lacy has already heard George's opinion of his family at the funeral: "They do nothing but die and marry and think about the honor of Virginia" (p. 107).

It is to save the Buchan family from themselves and their heroic principles that George takes upon himself the responsibility for the family estate. Convinced that the estate would break up sooner or later, he buys up the shares of Lacy's brothers and sells the family's "free" Negroes into slavery, thereby reducing Major Buchan's debt by a "couple of thousand dollars" (p. 131). To him the Major's own refusal to buy or sell a Negro was only a kind of fastidious self-indulgence at the expense of his posterity, who would have to sell the negroes sooner or later, or manumit them at the cost of actually giving the money away. I suppose George, in what was considered his high-handed fashion, took the first step against this family bankruptcy when he sold Jack Lewis and his family into Georgia: to have freed them, in deference to papa's wish, would have been, to George, to permit papa to rob his children in order to do what he considered humanly right" (p. 134).

This George could not accept, so he "somewhat characteristically" dealt with the family property—including Pleasant Hill, the country house—in terms of cash figures. "It was that sort of thing," Lacy says, "that annoyed Cousin John and irritated papa, who could not bring himself to think [that] the house that Dr. Buchan had built in 1791, 'for the enjoyment of the heirs forever,' not, mind you, for their profit, had any money value at all. If he admitted its money value he also admitted that it might some day be sold—which was unthinkable" (p. 134).

Though George Posey is not materialistic in any selfish sense, money is the one thing that seems to have a fixed value for him. His conduct therefore confounds the understanding of people like the Buchans who had never discussed money and "never asked how much money people had" (p. 135). For them "the individual quality of a man," Lacy recalls, "was bound up with his kin and the 'places' where they lived; thinking of a man we could easily bring before the mind's eye all those subtly interwoven features of his position. 'Class' consisted solely in a certain code of behavior," not in the way one made his money (p. 135). By not being a man of "honor and dignity," George Posey anticipates the future in which Lacy is narrating his story: "I knew gentlemen in my boyhood but I know none now," he says, "and I know that I am not one" (p. 210). Despite his own love for George, Lacy laments in part the loss of such gentlemen, with the simplicity and stability of their way of life: "They did a great deal of injustice but they always knew where they stood because they thought more of their code than they did of themselves" (p. 210).

In *The Fathers,* however, this loss is as inevitable as the coming of the Civil War. And George Posey serves to personify that inevitability throughout the novel: "Ain't I told you you can't do nothing' about hit?" the Major's manservant warns. "Ain't nobody kin stop that young gentleman, nobody" (p. 52). George forges through the events of Lacy's story as a solitary, irresistible intrusion of change into the established order of the Buchan world. Toward the end of the novel, Lacy imagines his dead grandfather telling him that "in my day we were never alone, as your brother-in-law is alone. He is alone like a tornado. His one purpose is to whirl and he brushes aside the obstacles in his way" (p. 268). Everything George does, in fact, betrays that solitude and motion; no one, not even his wife, seems to know anything about his business dealings. According to Lacy's Cousin John, "George would sell anything for the pleasure of buying something else; he had to keep moving" (p. 135). With no inherited code to order his own feelings and conduct, he remains a "wholly unprotected" figure. Thus, at Mrs. Buchan's funeral, he alone refuses to participate in the formal rituals of death that were to the Buchans, Lacy says, "only the completion of life, and in which there could be nothing personal, but in which what we were deep inside found a sufficient expression" (p. 23). So, too, George can impulsively kill Semmes Buchan and then try, in his unprecedented and "appallingly sincere" way, to explain his conduct to the Major.

Still, if George Posey is a "personal" force in a world whose "impersonality" he often cannot accept, it is also clear in *The Fathers* that he yearns somewhat nostalgically for the lost opportunities of his own youth, for the kind of social order and security represented by the Buchan way of life. In order "to cut a big dash among strangers" at the Fairfax tournament, he is willing to sell his Negro half-brother, Yellow Jim, for a big bay mare. And, though he sweeps Susan away from the tournament after a series of startling indiscretions, she remains his key to the closed doors of the Virginia aristocracy. Finally, George's "influence" on Semmes was not an influence, Lacy decides, "but an exchange in which each got from the other what he could not supply for himself" (p. 177). For Semmes it was "mystery and imagination, the heightened vitality possessed by a man who knew no bounds" (p. 179). Conversely,

> what Semmes gave to [George] was what he most needed but never could take: Semmes gave him first of all Susan, and then—papa being absolutely wrong about this—he tried to give him what the Poseys had lost: an idea, a cause, an action in which his personality could be extinguished, and it seemed as if George had succeeded in becoming a part of something greater than he: the Confederate cause. . . . In a world in which all men were like him, George would not have suffered—and he did suffer—the shock of communion with a world that he could not recover; while that world existed, its piety, its order, its elaborate rigamarole—his own forfeited heritage—teased him like a nightmare in which the dreamer dreams a dream within a dream within another dream of something that he cannot name (pp. 179, 180).

Eventually, George's attempt to regain his "forfeited heritage" turns into a legitimate nightmare when it clashes with his need to be free of any "enforced obligations." As his wife grows to fear the violence in his character, she becomes again a true Buchan and determines to prevent the imminent marriage between Semmes and Jane Posey, George's younger sister. Originally, Susan had been fascinated (like her brothers) by George's

> mysterious power, by his secrecy and his violence; but she wanted not power, nor secrecy, nor violence, except in so far as she could employ them to subdue those qualities in George Posey. She could not have known that George was outside life, or had a secret of life that no one had heard of at Pleasant Hill. To Susan the life around her in childhood had been final; there could be no other, there never had been any other way of life. . . . She could not have imagined a family that did not live by rigid order wherein everything meant something, whose meaning had been long agreed upon (pp. 183, 184).

In addition to the confusion and mystery of George's own personality, Susan has had to live with a house full of neurasthenic Poseys (mother, aunt, and uncle) whose "rather excessively refined sensibilities . . . had let their social tradition lapse in personal self-indulgence" (p. 184). Therefore, to prevent another Buchan-Posey marriage, Susan is willing even to permit Yellow Jim to rape Jane Posey (and, by accident, to frighten George's mother literally to death). But when Yellow Jim refuses to escape and throws himself on the mercy of his half-brother, Susan wildly attempts to force the obligation of revenge upon George rather than her brother Semmes. After Jane is rushed away to a convent and the men (and Lacy) convene in the Posey house, Susan gives her challenge:

> "Mr. Posey, you know what a fool my brother is." She looked at Semmes. "He would have shot any man for Mrs. Stacy and now he wants to shoot a negro for Jane Posey. Because he is a fool who happens to be a gentleman." She was a blazing fury as she rose to her feet. But her voice was low. "George Posey, if you allow my brother to shoot your brother for you, I will never see you again." She gazed into his wavering eyes (p. 253).

If Susan had not thus threatened her husband, Lacy thinks, George might have let Yellow Jim go or, perhaps, have killed him himself. But Semmes's presence had complicated the situation and hopelessly confused George. "There is reason to believe," Lacy decides,

> that when Susan threatened her husband she signed the death-warrant of her brother. George was infuriated. He was infuriated because he had been charged with a definite responsibility, by somebody else: he had been told what to do. It was too much for him. From the minute he left Susan's bedroom I cannot believe that he meant to kill Yellow Jim. Without thinking it through he had, up to then, assumed that he would kill him, or at least he was prepared to take him out and to go through the motions of disposing of him (p. 271).

Not even the additional horror of his mother having died the same night can shock George into the acceptance of a superior duty: if he had been able to step across the threshhold into the parlor where her body lay, as he was about to leave the house on his supposed errand of vengeance, then perhaps, Lacy thinks, George might not have escorted his half-brother to his death. But, at that point,

> he was between two fires of enforced obligation, and there was one of them that was so bright, unequivocal, and compelling—his dead mother—that if for no other reason than that he would have taken Yellow Jim up the river (p. 271).

George will not have any obligation forced upon him; and, if people or events conspire to do so, he will choose the lesser of two obligations or do nothing at all.

It is Semmes who finally kills Yellow Jim and George who turns on his brother-in-law. His anguished revelation—"I never had any idea of killing that nigger" (p. 258)—Lacy realizes, is the self-discovery of a man with no alternative code of conduct to oppose the Buchan "logic" of retribution. In his moment of tragic indecision, blood (in the person of Yellow Jim) remains thicker than water (his sympathies with Semmes), but not thick enough to prevent the death of either man. George's marriage to Susan, rather than bringing order out of the disorder of his own life, as he had hoped, only results in the imposition of his disorder and violence upon the Buchan family.

The last act of Lacy's story is an account of George Posey's belated attempt to "be with the men" fighting the war—to make "your people" his people. But, again, George can not act impersonally; as the Battle of Bull Run is about to begin, he is insulted by an old enemy and promptly kills him. Returning, then, to Pleasant Hill, George and Lacy find the old house burned to the ground and Major Buchan dead by his own hand. It is, for George, a final display of the "wilful and arbitrary" absurdity behind the self-destruction of the Buchan family. To the end, he can not comprehend how a man like the Major could be, above all, polite to the Yankee who is threatening his life and property. George would at least have hit him (as, in fact, he earlier did) rather than turn his violence upon himself.

George's last gesture is to remove the Confederate uniform

(which he leaves, symbolically, in a heap upon the ground) and to ride off, alone, into the growing darkness. "I waited," Lacy says, "until I heard the change of the hoofbeats on the big road. I kicked the old nag in the sides and headed back into the lane that ran by the south field" (p. 306). Then, for the first and last time in *The Fathers,* Lacy the narrator becomes one with Lacy the boy (as the past tense changes to the present): "I'll go back and finish it. I'll have to finish it because he could not finish it. It won't make any difference if I am killed. If I am killed it will be because I love him more than I love any man" (p. 306). Though it is too late for George himself to change, to turn back the clock, it is not too late, this once, for Lacy in his old age to judge what has happened to him. He must "finish" not only George's attempt to fight in the war, his effort to define himself according to something greater than himself, but he must also, with the acknowledgment of his love, live out his own life as the historical offspring of George's confusion and disorder, as a member of the changing world "that had been created by George Posey, out of the dead world of my mother"(p. 13).

9

"The price had been necessity": William Faulkner's *The Hamlet*

When one considers the juxtaposition of nostalgia and social change in the novels of William Faulkner, *The Sound and the Fury* usually comes to mind, although in that novel, as in most of Faulkner's work, "there is alway something else . . . more arresting than the observation of manners."[1] This is least of all the case, however, in *The Hamlet* (the first of the Snopes trilogy), which also deals with nostalgia and social change, but in a broader and more "realistic" context than does *The Sound and the Fury*. Beside the obvious difference in focus between the two novels—that is, the family as opposed to the larger community—Faulkner's tone in *The Hamlet,* thanks in part to the absence of the first-person point of view, is more detached and more ironic. In either novel, however, the basis for Faulkner's irony can be better understood with the help of the following passage from Richard Chase's *The American Novel and Its Tradition;* speaking of *The Sound and the Fury,* Chase concluded that

> readers who follow the traditionalist view of Faulkner will have trouble seeing Jason as Faulkner sees him. I mean by the "traditionalist view" that kind of conservative criticism that divides Faulkner's characters into Sartorises (good) and

142

Snopeses (bad). The good people, according to this account, retain the Southern ideals of honor and justice; they believe in a society based on tradition, religion, and the sense of community. The bad people are individualistic materialists who have no conception of honor, tradition, or the sanctity of family and community, whose only notion of community is, in fact, the cash nexus.

There is no doubt that these moral distinctions are important to Faulkner, as they are for any thinking person. Presumably he would like to accept them in their pristine "Confederate" innocence, were he not too modern, too realistic, and too honest to do so. He accepts them, one may think, but with all the reservation and irony which a divided and contradictory mind is likely to exhibit.[2]

If such moral distinctions are obscure in *The Sound and the Fury,* they are even more so in *The Hamlet,* where the conflict between the Snopeses and the Southern "sense of community" is more explicit. Frenchman's Bend, after all, has its own thieves and con men—the Varners, whose manners Flem Snopes is determined to imitate:

> the clerk [Snopes] now lived in the village. . . . He who had never been seen in the village between Saturday night and Monday morning appeared at the church, and those who saw him looked at him for an instant in incredulous astonishment. In addition to the gray cloth cap and the gray trousers, he wore not only a clean white shirt but a necktie—a tiny machine-made black bow which snapped together at the back with a metal fastener. It was not two inches long and with the exception of the one which Will Varner himself wore to church it was the only tie in the Frenchman's Bend country, and from that Sunday morning until the day he died he wore it or one just like it . . . which gave him Jody Varner's look of ceremonial heterodoxy raised to its tenth power. . . .[3]

Flem's eventual succession to the ownership of the old mansion is a further manifestation of the economic tyranny that has traditionally characterized Frenchman's Bend. The opening pages of the novel, for example, make it perfectly clear that what follows has, in some sense, already happened before: Flem Snopes's conquest of the village is just the latest in a series of power shifts. The Old Frenchman's place—the "gutted ruin" of a large pre-Civil War plantation—is the symbol of a more fertile past and has at that time (c. 1890) passed into the hands of Will Varner, replete with fallen stables and legends of money buried somewhere about the property. At least once every month, Faulkner says, Will Varner "would be seen by someone sitting in a home-made chair on the jungle-choked lawn of the Old Frenchman's homesite . . . chewing his tobacco or smoking his cob pipe, with a brusque word for passers cheerful enough but inviting no company, against his background of fallen baronial splendor" (p. 6). "I like to set here, " he tells V. K. Ratliff. "I'm trying to find out what it must have felt like to be the fool that would need all this just to eat and sleep in. . . .I reckon I'll just keep what there is left of it, just to remind me of my one mistake. This is the only thing I ever bought in my life I couldn't sell to nobody" (p. 7). For his part, however, Ratliff "never for one moment believed that it had no value" (p. 179); so, when Varner finally does let it go, to Flem Snopes, Ratliff is convinced that

> it was because Varner had at last got the price for which he had been holding it for twenty years, or at least some sufficient price, whether it was in money or not. And when he considered who Varner had relinquished possession to, he believed that the price had been necessity and not cash (p. 180).

Flem Snopes becomes the inevitable recipient of Varner's most prized possessions because, in one sense, he plays the trading game better than his native counterparts (later he makes his profit on the mansion by pawning it off on Ratliff, among others). His "dispassionate and imperturbable" consistency is the perfection of a type already familiar to the inhabitants of Frenchman's Bend. Thus Snopes, out of his own profit instinct, can play upon the same envy and greed in the weaker townspeople, of which the spotted-horses episode is the pièce de résistance. Though he irresistibly disrupts the established order of the village, his financial success depends upon its double standard of judgment, its own "separation of economic and personal ethics."[4]

But granting these moral continuities, there are further and more important discontinuities between Snopes and the village of Frenchman's Bend that account, to a great extent, for Faulkner's realism and irony in *The Hamlet*. Put another way, the fact of continuity is subsumed under a larger historical vision of discontinuity and change. There is something in the last analysis very alien about Flem Snopes that confounds the accustomed habits of thought and action in Frenchman's Bend. He vanquishes all opposition not only because he understands and uses the villagers' moral weaknesses, but also because they, for their part, are constitutionally unable to understand and cope with the sociohistorical phenomenon that he represents. He becomes, for Faulkner, not merely the latest manifestation of historical change but also a personification of history itself—that ineluctable, amoral process of change that never allows people to rest easy with their established myths and rituals (or even with their traditional processes of change). As such, the question of a moral attitude toward Flem Snopes is as irrelevant, in the end, as the villagers' attempt to resist him is futile; Snopes's rise in *The Hamlet* is presented as if it were, in Irving Howe's words, "somehow beyond help or judgment and nothing could be done but to witness and even relish the catastrophe."[5] Clearly, Faulkner nostalgically preferred a community like pre-Snopes Frenchman's Bend, based on barter rather than profit, on the products of the soil rather than the gold that might be hidden in it, on a social existence that is somehow "natural" rather than artificial and man-made. But Faulkner's vision of history also told him that the natural would inevitably give way in time to the artificial and that to resist this fact only increased one's self-deception and hastened one's self-defeat.[6] He therefore leaves the burden of nostalgia to his characters.

The central historical conflict in *The Hamlet* is between a communal way of life that is, in general, passive, verbal, and ritualistic and a noncommunal way of life that is, by contrast, active, wordless, and irreverent. Flem Snopes embodies the latter. But the Varners and V. K. Ratliff, despite their own shrewdness, belong to the larger community, whose primary institution is the eternal gathering of men on the gallery of Varner's store. (At one point in the novel it seems to Ratliff, after returning to Frenchman's Bend, that "the same men who had been there when he saw it last a year ago were still sitting" on the gallery [pp. 87–88].) Again and again, Faulkner brings the reader back to Varner's store, where much is said about the Snopeses and little is done to resist their presence. On the other hand, Flem Snopes himself says almost nothing in the course of the novel (approximately 260 words spread over eighteen pages) and is repeatedly characterized as secretive about his business or silent in the presence of Jody Varner's volubility. Even in the novel's final scene, when Armstid is digging frantically for gold on the property that Snopes has salted, the antithesis between the verbal rituals of the village and the silence that surrounds Flem Snopes provides Faulkner's main image of contrast:

> In the hot summer mornings, squatting with slow tobacco or snuff-sticks on the gallery of Varner's store, or at quiet cross-roads about the land in the long slant of afternoon, they talked about it, wagon to wagon, wagon to rider, rider to rider or from wagon or rider to one waiting beside a mailbox or a gate: "Is he [Armstid] still at it?"
> "He's still at it."
> "He's going to kill himself. Well, I don't know as it will be any loss."
> "Not to his wife, anyway."
> "That's a fact. It will save her that trip every day toting food to him. That Flem Snopes."
> "That's a fact. Wouldn't no other man have done it" (pp. 419–20).

But when Snopes passes the field where Armstid is digging, the watchers keep silent:

> he drove on past the halted wagons while the heads of the women holding the nursing children turned to look at him and the heads of the men along the fence turned to watch him pass, the faces grave, veiled too, still looking at him when he

stopped the wagon and sat, chewing with that steady and measured thrust and looking over their heads into the garden. Then the heads along the ruined fence turned as though to follow his look. . . . The people watched [Armstid] in a silence so complete that they could hear the dry whisper of his panting breath (p. 420).

Will Varner, and all that he possesses or that bears his name, is the primary object of Flem Snopes's conquest. As Faulkner describes him, Varner is

the chief man of the country. He was the largest landholder and beat supervisor in one county and Justice of the Peace in the next and election commissioner in both, and hence the fountainhead if not of law at least of advice and suggestion to a countryside which would have repudiated the term constituency if they had ever heard of it. . . . He was a farmer, a usurer, a veterinarian; Judge Benbow of Jefferson once said of him that a milder-mannered man never bled a mule or stuffed a ballot box. He owned most of the good land in the country and held mortgages on most of the rest. He owned the store and the cotton gin and the combined grist mill and blacksmith shop in the village proper and it was considered, to put it mildly, bad luck for a man of the neighborhood to do his trading or gin his cotton or grind his meal or shoe his stock anywhere else (pp. 5–6).

Yet, as dishonest and shrewd as he may be, Will Varner's kind of power in Yoknapatawpha County is of a different order than that of Flem Snopes. At the heart of his operation is the belief, expressed by Jody, that one needs "the good will of the folks he aims to make his money off of" (p. 26). Thus, the Varner store is run on a certain amount of trust between the absent owner and the customers, who "would enter and serve themselves and each other, putting the price of the articles, which they knew to a penny as well as Jody himself did, into a cigar box inside the circular wire cage which protected the cheese" (p. 28). Little things are of no great importance to the Varners; with the other "profoundly idle" villagers, Will Varner shares "the curse of his own invincible conviction of the absolute unimportance of this or any other given moment or succession of them" (p. 121).

In the opening chapter of the novel, however, it is obvious that the Varners must deal with an antagonist who, unlike themselves, has no concern for public opinion (though he does in the later Snopes stories). Before Jody, for example, can extort a season's crop from his new tenant, Ab Snopes, by threatening him with the knowledge of his having burned a neighboring barn in the past, his son Flem humbles Jody by blackmailing him with the threat of another fire. What Jody can not comprehend is that other men can be oblivious to accepted social concepts such as the importance of one's reputation and the purposelessness of violence. For some Snopeses in *The Hamlet*—Flem's father and his impoverished cousin Mink in particular—the recourse to violence seems to invite retribution; but Flem himself successfully functions according to a theory of power unknown in Frenchman's Bend: personal aggrandizement through the use of fear, rather than the use of good will. When Jody Varner was clerk in the family store, he had given the townspeople all the credit they needed, "though they knew they would pay interest for that which on its face looked like generosity and openhandedness, whether that interest showed in the final discharge or not" (pp. 64–65). But when Flem takes over, they discover that there will be no more credit of any kind for anyone. "He [Snopes] finally flatly refused further credit to a man who had been into and out of the store's debt at least once a year for the last fifteen" (p. 65). Even Will Varner must pay for a plug of tobacco from his own store.

No longer is the economic existence of Frenchman's Bend based upon a mutual acceptance of human weakness. The villagers "can't wait to bare their backsides" to the Snopeses, as Ratliff puts it, because the Snopes concept of the human community will not allow them to remain both happy and passive (thus, they must spend weeks chasing the same spotted horses that they couldn't resist buying from Snopes in the first place). In their determination to believe the spotted horses are of value, the men sitting on Varner's gallery form a perfect image of the entire village's inevitable inability to resist the wiles of Flem Snopes: "there seemed to gather about the three silhouettes," Faulkner says, "something stubborn, convinced, and passive, like children who have been chidden" (p. 317).

The impotence of Frenchman's Bend before the new historical phenomenon represented by Flem Snopes is the basis for the comedy and pathos of *The Hamlet,* and nowhere is this more evident than in the second section of the novel—"Eula"—and, specifically, in the "shabby and fustian gallantry" of Jody Varner. Eula, his teenage sister, is the town's symbol, paradoxically, of both fertility and virginity: sitting "supine and female and soft and immovable," she suggests "that ungirdled quality of the very goddesses in . . . Homer and Thucycides: of being at once corrupt and immaculate, at once virgins and the mothers of warriors and of grown men" (pp. 111, 128). She is the focus of the villagers' impotence, their desire both to protect and ravish the natural order that she seems to personify. For example, in the mind of Labove, Eula's anguished schoolteacher, she becomes inextricably associated with "the fine land rich and fecund and foul and eternal and impervious to him who claimed title to it" (p. 135). The earth, in this sense, is one of the forces in *The Hamlet* that keeps men impotent against their will, that produces man, as Faulkner says in reference to Armstid, "to be its born and fated thrall forever until he died" (p. 413); and Eula Varner, in her person, arouses an antagonism in the men who hopelessly seek to conquer her virginity, as they do the land that manages to keep them poor. But, for the men of Frenchman's Bend in particular, Eula Varner also embodies the kind of timeless, unself-conscious existence that they envision, nostalgically, for their entire community. Like the Old Frenchman's Place, she becomes an image for them of a more fertile past and is, therefore, a particularly symbolic acquisition for Flem Snopes. In one of his more rhetorical and poetic passages, Faulkner describes the town and its attitude toward Eula as

> a little lost village, nameless, without grace, forsaken, yet which wombed once by chance and accident one blind seed of the spendthrift Olympian ejaculation and did not even know it, without tumescence conceived, and bore . . . a word, a single will to believe born of envy and old deathless

regret, . . . the word, the dream and wish of all male under sun capable of harm . . . the word, with its implications of lost triumphs and defeats of unimaginable splendor—and which best: to have that word, that dream and hope for future, or to have had need to flee that word and dream, for past (p. 169).

In her inviolable fertility, Eula is the wishful self-image of the village, at once the symbol of its present frustration, its future possibilities, and its past triumphs. In marrying her (out of convenience, of course, not love, since she is pregnant by another man), Flem Snopes symbolically robs the village of all three: past, present, and future. Morally, his is the final rape of Frenchman's Bend; historically, it is the inevitable defeat of a village whose very way of life is founded, to begin with, upon its own nostalgic illusions and feelings of impotence (toward time, on the one hand, and Nature, on the other). Both the virginity and fertility of life in Frenchman's Bend were doomed long before the arrival of Flem Snopes; thus the sense of calm inevitability that pervades the scene at the end of book two when Flem Snopes wordlessly marries Eula, for which Will Varner gives him the wedding license, a honeymoon in Texas, and the Old Frenchman's Place.

No one seeks to protect Eula from her eventual fate—pregnancy and marriage—as much as Jody Varner; he, more than anyone else in Faulkner's novel, represents an incestuous resistance to the realities of time and change comically reminiscent of Quentin Compson in *The Sound and the Fury.* In his introduction of Jody, for example, Faulkner gives him "an air not funereal exactly but ceremonial," thanks to "that quality of invincible bachelorhood which he possessed":

> so that, looking at him you saw, beyond the flabbiness and the obscuring bulk, the perennial and immortal Best Man, the apotheosis of the masculine Singular, just as you discern beneath the dropsical tissue of the '09 halfback the lean hard ghost which once carried a ball (p. 8).

Jody is the primal bachelor, the "jealous seething eunuch priest," as Faulkner later calls him (p. 130), whose job it becomes to take

his child-woman sister back and forth to school twice a day over
the half mile she refused to walk; then,

> she would slide off the horse and her brother would sit for a
> moment longer, seething, watching the back which already
> used its hips to walk with as women used them, and speculate
> with raging impotence whether to call the schoolteacher (he
> was a man) outside at once and have it out with him, warn or
> threaten or even use his fists, or whether to wait until that
> happened which he, Varner, was convinced must occur (p.
> 114).

It is Jody, too, who nags his phlegmatic mother into making Eula
wear corsets, after which "he would grasp her each time he saw
her outside the house, in public or alone, and see for himself if
she had them on" (p. 148). When she finally becomes pregnant,
despite his efforts, Jody is barely restrained by his father from
pursuing the culprit to Texas and defending the Varner name.
The irony, of course, is that Jody is jousting at windmills, while
Flem Snopes, in marrying Eula, is once again responsible for the
actual devaluation of Varner power and respectability. Unable
to resist Snopes himself, Jody can only oppose those other members of the community who, in their lust for the glorious shame
of violating Eula, will eventually make possible another acquisition of used property by Flem Snopes.

Jody Varner is not the only major character in *The Hamlet*
spoken of specifically in terms of celibacy or impotence. After
teaching in Eula Varner's presence for five years, the frustrated
Labove, for example, became "the monk indeed, the bleak
schoolhouse, the little barren village, was his mountain, his
Gethsemane and, he knew it, his Golgotha too. He was the virile
anchorite of old time" (p. 134). Similarly, confronted with the
love affair between Ike Snopes and his cow, the farmer Houston
feels a helpless rage at the circumstances that force him to "return and establish once more physical contact with the female
world" which he had abjured with the death of his wife three
years before (p. 214). Even the sewing-machine agent, V. K.
Ratliff, whom one critic has called "Faulkner's most sympathetic

and intelligent observer,"[7] is given that "same air of perpetual bachelorhood which Jody Varner had," although in Ratliff it is meant to be the "hearty celibacy as of a lay brother in a twelfth-century monastery—a gardener, a pruner of vines, say" (p. 48). This sympathetic description, however, is not entirely supported by Ratliff's role in the novel: if he is an intelligent observer, he is not a detached observor, and if he is a "hearty" celibate, he also shares some of Jody's, Labove's, and Houston's impotence. His own overconfidence in his ability to "risk fooling with" Flem Snopes and his moral outrage at Snopes's apparent invulnerability distinguish Ratliff's attitudes from the more resigned position of the author and prepare the reader for the final section of the novel, in which Ratliff's purchase of the Old Frenchman's Place completes Snopes's conquest of the village.

Behind Ratliff's "faint constant humorous mask" (p. 92) and his gibes about the helplessness of the other villagers ("So Flem has come home again. Well, well, well. Will Varner paid to get him to Texas, so I reckon it aint no more than fair for you fellows to pay the freight on him back" [p. 315]), there is a personal interest in the defeat of Flem Snopes. He considers himself the only man other than Will Varner who might be able to outsmart Snopes (pp. 31, 101); and the incident in which Snopes buys the fifty goats and resells them to Ratliff (thus cutting Ratliff's profit from $20 to $5 and making $7.50 for himself) only serves to whet Ratliff's hopes of victory. His sympathy for the idiot Ike Snopes and for Mink's wife and children, of course, accounts for some of his outrage. But much of it is also the result of his being a full-fledged member of the passive, verbal, and ritualistic society of Frenchman's Bend and the caretaker, in effect, of its nostalgic self-image.

As Faulkner portrays him, Ratliff is the local storyteller and courier. On his first trip outside his regular territory in ten years, he sells eight sewing-machines in a month and finds himself "shut away from his native state by a golden barrier, a wall of neatly accumulating minted coins" (p. 62). By contrast, within his "established and nurtured round of newsmongering," Ratliff sells only about three machines a year, while the rest of the time trading in land and livestock and second-hand farming tools and musical instruments or anything else which the owner did not want badly enough, retailing from house to house the news of his four counties with the ubiquity of a newspaper and carrying personal messages from mouth to mouth about weddings and funerals and the preserving of vegetables and fruit with the reliability of a postal service (pp. 62, 15).

In a sense, Ratliff is the acknowledged spokesman for the rural society in which he moves; the confusion and outrage of others, therefore, gives the occasion for his own opposition to Flem Snopes. He, too, feels that Eula Varner should at the last "have been the unscalable sierra, the rosy virginal mother of barricades for no man to conquer scot-free or even to conquer at all" (p. 181). And after Flem Snopes has managed to conquer her "scot-free," Ratliff shares the town's outrage at what seems to him

the waste, the useless squandering; at a situation intrinsically and inherently wrong by any economy, like building a log dead-fall and baiting it with a freshened heifer to catch a rat; or no, worse: as though the gods themselves had funnelled all the concentrated bright wet-slanted unparadised June onto a dung-heap, breeding pismires (p. 182).

Later, Ratliff's anger is expressed verbally on the gallery when he talks, always in his quiet imperturbable manner, about Will Varner's "stern getting reamed out" by the Snopeses in "this here best of all possible worlds" (p. 185) and then, in Snopes's presence, about Mrs. Armstid's need to get her five dollars from Flem Snopes after he returns "from wherever he has been since the auction [of the spotted horses], which of course," he adds sarcastically, "is to town naturally to see about his cousin [Mink] that's got into a little legal trouble" (p. 359).

Ratliff's own victimization by Flem Snopes's trick of salting the earth with hidden treasure, in the last section of the novel, is consistent with his prior characterization. His collapse is needed, to be sure, to "round off" Flem's triumph, but it also reflects

Ratliff's continually paradoxical attitude toward Snopes: his belief, on the one hand, in Flem's power (that he could somehow
"persuade" Will Varner to relinquish the old mansion with its
secret assets), and his hope, on the other hand, that he—V. K.
Ratliff—might some day beat the master at his own game. When
Flem Snopes moves into Jefferson in *The Town,* published seventeen years after *The Hamlet,* Ratliff fades into the background of
Faulkner's story and is obviously, as Irving Howe has said, "a
figure from an earlier time and another kind of life who is not
really at home in the present moment."[8] This is already evident,
however, in *The Hamlet,* to the extent that Ratliff voices the nostalgic frustration and defends the self-image of Frenchman's
Bend.

The central phenomenon in *The Hamlet* is a social, historical
phenomenon, and all the other stories in the novel (particularly
in "The Long Summer" section dealing with Ike, Houston, and
Mink Snopes) are secondary to the drama of Flem Snopes's
"usurpation of an heirship" in Frenchman's Bend (p. 101).
Whatever humor there is in the novel, and there is a great deal
indeed, is the direct consequence of Flem's undeflected will and
of the extraordinary ratio between what the inhabitants of
Frenchman's Bend *say* (usually on Varner's gallery) and what
they *do.* V. K. Ratliff is, in one sense, the wit, conscience, and
gadfly of this community ("I can't even get nowhere in time to
buy a cheap horse" [p. 351]), but, in a larger sense, he is as much
a part of the community as an Armstid or a Varner; discounting
his private impenetrability, he readily conforms to Faulkner's
image of life in Yoknapatawpha County as, day in and day out, a
kind of static set-piece:

On successive days and two counties apart the splashed and
battered buckboard and the strong mismatched team might be
seen tethered in the nearest shade and Ratliff's bland affable
ready face and his neat tieless blue shirt one of the squatting
group at a crossroads store, or—and still squatting and still
doing the talking apparently though actually doing a good
deal   more   listening   than   anyone   believed   until
afterward—among the women surrounded by laden clothes-

lines and tubs and blackened wash pots beside springs and
wells, or decorous in a splint chair on cabin galleries, pleasant,
affable, courteous, anecdotal . . . (pp. 14–15).

The passive and timeless permanence suggested by this passage
is the quality that Flem Snopes exploits and history must inevitably alter.

10

"The lost and impossible miles": A. B. Guthrie, Jr.'s
These Thousand Hills

A. B. Guthrie, Jr.'s four novels about the settlement of the American West (the Rocky Mountain region to the Pacific) all deal with social change and nostalgia. Taken together, *The Big Sky, The Way West, These Thousand Hills,* and *Arfive* present a vision of history based upon the hopelessness of resisting progress and the disappointment of embracing it: "changes come on, regardless," the wisest of Guthrie's characters says in *The Big Sky.* In the second novel, the same character—a former trapper and present scout for a wagon train—elaborates on the same point:

Summers thought it was only the earth that didn't change. It was just the mountains, watching others flower and seed, watching men come and go, the Indian first and after him the trapper, pushing up the unspoiled rivers, pleased with risk and loneliness, and now the wanters of new homes, the hunters of fortune, the would-be makers of a bigger nation, spelling the end to a time that was ended anyway.

He didn't blame the Oregoners as he had known old mountain men to do. Everybody had his life to make, and every time its way, one different from another. The fur hunter didn't have title to the mountains no matter if he did say finders' keepers. By that system the country belonged to the Indians, or maybe someone before them or someone before them. No use to stand against the stream of change and time.[1]

The trapper, or mountain man, during the 1830s is the subject of *The Big Sky,* and the first settlers who followed in the 1840s are the subject of *The Way West,* which won a Pulitzer Prize for Guthrie in 1950. As such, these novels are very similar—in spirit as well as subject matter—to the first two volumes of a historical trilogy by another Pulitzer Prize winner: Bernard DeVoto's *Across the Wide Missouri* and *The Year of Decision: 1846.* If Guthrie specialized in historical fiction, then DeVoto, at his best, wrote a kind of imaginative history, both attempting to envision and dramatize a process of historical change that was romantic in its scope yet often very unromantic in its results. One could argue that Guthrie and DeVoto were themselves somewhat nostalgic in their desire to recapture the spirit of the American West, whether that spirit resulted in fulfillment (in *The Way West*), disappointment (in *The Big Sky*), or both (in *Arfive,* which deals with Montana in the early 1900s). Like DeVoto, who became his friend and a promoter of his novels in the 1940s, Guthrie spent his boyhood years in the West (Montana as opposed to Utah) and then wrote from the other side of the Mississippi out of a fondness for the dreams of those historical figures who wanted the West to be, ultimately, something unhistorical and even mythical. Indeed, in his own fiction, Guthrie may well be said to approximate one of Wallace Stegner's descriptions of DeVoto:

> Debunking or correcting western myths, scorning the things the West had become, he would continue to love, to the point of passion, western openness, freedom, air, scenery, violence; and would accept some of the myths as eagerly as the most illiterate cowhand reading *Western Stories* in the shade of the cookhouse.[2]

But this is least true of *These Thousand Hills,* which is also, artistically, Guthrie's best novel (despite his own disclaimer that it was his "most difficult and least successful [novel], because it dealt with the cowpuncher and had to avoid, if it could, the stylized western myth"[3]). The concern with social change is still there—in this case, the homesteading and fencing of open range by the first cattlemen in Montana during the 1880s. But Guthrie's nostalgia (as distinguished from that of his characters) had been toned down. In DeVoto's histories, nostalgia had been, in Stegner's words, a "release of dammed images, memories, feelings" that was necessary for an "imaginative recreation of the frontier."[4] In *The Big Sky* and *The Way West,* on the other hand, despite their reception and popularity, the author's nostalgia often became an artistic liability. There, Guthrie's narrative technique was to voice, alternately and often in separate chapters, the unexpressed thoughts of his various characters (as, for example, in the passage above describing Summers's thinking). The problem with Guthrie's use of a literary convention like this is that his prose became inflated and sentimental whenever the feelings of a particular character became inflated and sentimental. The following passages from *The Big Sky* and *The Way West,* respectively, are typical:

> [Summers] wanted to be by himself, to go along alone with the emptiness that was in him, to look and listen and see and smell, . . . feeling the night press in around him, seeing the stars wink and the dipper steady, and everything saying good-bye, goodbye.
>   Goodbye, Dick Summers. Goodbye, you old nigger, you. We mind the time you came to us, young and green and full of sap. We watched you grow into a proper mountain man. We saw you learning, trapping and fighting, and finding trails, and going around then proud-breasted like a young rooster, ready for a frolic or a fracas, your arm strong and your wind sound and the squaws proud to have you under a robe. But new times are a-coming now, and new people, a heap of them, and wheels rolling over the passes, carrying greenhorns and women and maybe children, too, and plows. The old days are gone and beaver's through. We'll see a sight of change, but not you, Dick Summers. The years have fixed you. Time to go now. Time to give up. Time to sit back and remember. Time for a chair and a bed. Time to wait to die. Goodbye, Dick. Goodbye, Old Man Summers.[5]

Evans told himself that if any train could get to Oregon, this

one could. It had the best pilot that he knew of, best man and
pilot both. Its stock was poor but no poorer than would come
behind. Its wagons were as good as others would be by the
time they reached the ford. But it was the men he counted on,
the men and women and spirit of the company. They had
their faults, he knew. They had their differences and sometimes spoke severe, what with sand in their teeth and worries
in their heads, but they wished well for one another and they
hung together. Here where sometimes he'd heard the trains
split up, old On-to-Oregon stayed one. Looking down the line
from head to tail after the long drop to the Snake came into
sight, he felt a kind of wrathy pride. Damn the Snake and all
its sorry kin of sage and sand! Damn the crossing! They'd
make it—he and Summers and Patch and Mack and
Daugherty and Shields and Gorham and all the rest, clear
down to Byrd. They'd make it or go down trying and still
damn the Snake to do its damnedest.[6]

The prose in *These Thousand Hills* is, on the whole, far more
precise and restrained than this. Guthrie seldom uses the technique of recording, chapter by chapter, each character's
thoughts and feelings (which he uses again, consistently, in
Arfive), relying far more on the dramatic action of the novel to
represent specific ideas and emotions. This is due in part, but
not primarily, to the fact that the subject of *These Thousand Hills*
is more social in nature than the subjects of *The Big Sky* and *The
Way West,* that is, more dependent upon dialogue and interac-
tion among characters. In addition, however, the narrative language in *These Thousand Hills,* discounting dialogue, is less collo-
quial and affected than in Guthrie's other novels, with the author himself assuming a more detached and dispassionate point
of view. The comparison between Montana and Oregon, for
example, in their meanings for Lat Evans, Guthrie's central
character, is brought out in a conversation between Evans and
an interested banker, rather than in the kind of reverie quoted
above:

Out of the chance, unconnected bits of his thought he was
asked now, all at once, to sum up and come out with answers.
He got a pinchhold of one. "First of all, Mr. Conrad, I see the

time when grasslands will have to be owned or anyhow leased."

"You see a long way. There'll be free graze in Montana for longer than you'll ever live. Uncrowded graze."

"That's your notion!" With the words out he almost wished he hadn't spoken so strongly. Conrad was an older man and a banker besides. But he still could be wrong. "They said the same thing in eastern Oregon not so far back."

"Yes?"

"And now ranges are so crowded that cattle half-starve and some ranchers think heifers and cows should be spayed. Smart men are putting land under fence, owned land and leased land. Costs money, but it pays off. The cattle get feed. And the cows don't mix with scrub bulls."[7]

Only in the first four chapters of *These Thousand Hills* (out of thirty-seven) and intermittently thereafter does Guthrie adhere strictly to the dominant consciousness and private thoughts of a single character for any length of time, and then in nearly every instance it is Lat Evans. Though no less important than in Guthrie's other novels, the dreams of the characters in *These Thousand Hills,* nostalgic or otherwise, are implicit in the drama of the novel rather than explicit in its language, thus obviating the problem of distinguishing the author's own attitudes from the romanticizing of his characters.

Specifically, the dramatic situation of the novel is developed through five episodes in the life of Lat Evans, each comprising a section of the novel and together covering a period of seven years, from 1880 to 1887. The first section recounts Lat's journey on a cattle drive from the Oregon home of his father (the boy Brownie in *The Way West*) to Fort Benton, Montana; the second section covers his "wolfing" expedition the following winter and his wounding, capture, and release by a roving band of Indians; the third, his convalescence in a Fort Benton whorehouse, his "unpropitious" love affair with a prostitute named Callie Kash, and his lucrative victory in a horse race; the fourth, three years later, his success at ranching and his "respectable" involvement in the economic and social future of Tansytown, near Fort Benton; and the last section, after four more years and his marriage to the niece of a leading citizen, his participation in a vigilante raid against cattle thieves and his decision to reveal his past to his wife and testify as a character witness when Callie, by then the madam of a whorehouse, is suspected in a murder.

The ironic moral of this story is stated, wistfully, by Lat's grandfather—the leader of the pioneers in *The Way West*—at the beginning of the novel: "A man likes to grow up with the country. And when he gets growed up, he likes the country growed up, too. Or maybe he does or maybe he don't. Some ways one way, some ways t'other" (p. 9). The one character who is aware of the irony in this statement—that social change can neither be avoided nor fully appreciated—is Colly, an old prospector and family friend; his single piece of advice to Lat, before he leaves on the cattle drive, is a practical observation about ranching that later makes Lat a success and forces him to face the fact that, like it or not, the country is going to grow up and that he will have to grow up in his own way under *new* social circumstances. In one sense, Lat would like to escape the past and the economic failure represented by his father and by the Oregon territory that once had been a promised land for his family, but has become "spoiled" by "too many people, too much stock, too many homestead claims" (p. 3). In another sense, however, Lat wants to relive the past—this time in Montana—and make the myth that motivated his grandfather finally come true:

> He'd own cattle, and by the thousands, and have range for them in the new land of Montana, and men would come to him to ask advice, all brands and breeds of men, including some who wouldn't go to Pa; and Pa would smile a proud, small smile, since he hadn't done as well, and say, "We knew it from the first, son" (pp. 16–17).

Thus, Lat's eastern journey "backwards along the road that Pa and Grandpa had helped grind out so long before" (p. 12) is a journey in time as well as space.

At age twenty, Lat is yet naive about the aspirations of men.

Passing the stream of emigrants still going to Oregon, he makes light of their strenuous hopes:

> They'd find the good soil taken up, the ranges worked, cabins here and there and yonder, the cows and sheep they drove at so much pains not worth the trailing, and no grass to feed them on to boot. So the last would be the worst, the measly answer to the toilsome hope (p. 18).

But Ram Butler, the trail boss, sees that Lat is identifying, in his bitterness, with the latest pioneers and reminds him that reality always falls short of one's aspirations, no matter how admirable they may be:

> It's new land to 'em and so won't be a come-down for a spell. Most folks don't like to stick. What's yondeh beats what's nigh. . . . It's only by and by that what they left looks good, and then because it's wheah they ain't (p. 18).

Simply stated, Lat would like to believe that the hardships of living and the mutability of history can be transcended, at least in his own case. These later travelers, he thinks,

> had it easy until the very last when they would find not milk and honey the land they strained for now. It never had been, for that matter, else Pa would have some money, wouldn't he? Else Ma could fix and prettify the house like she'd always wanted to and like she would in time.

And Lat imagines himself back home years later saying,

> "Do everything you want, Ma, and in the way you want it. Money is no object." And, standing by, Pa seemed shaken in his belief that it was hard for a rich man to enter the Kingdom of Heaven (p. 18).

Thus from the continental divide, Montana appears to Lat as Oregon appeared to his father and grandfather thirty-five years before: a boundless Promised Land of grass and sky.

Here, at the outset of his adventure as a pioneer, Lat fails to realize that the significance of Montana for him is divided and contradictory. On the one hand, its distances and openness evoke in him a positive sense of freedom and fundamental permanence, "like standing on top of the world," he says (p. 240). On the other hand, the same virgin prairie, the "miles endless and vacant, allowed chances and choices beyond all reasonable hope . . . as Oregon must have before crowds wore the trail to it deep. All that was needed," he thinks, "was cattle or money for cattle" (p. 107). To be a successful rancher, however, necessitates, quite literally in terms of fences and irrigation ditches, the division and destruction of openness and of the sense of freedom that comes of openness. And not until the final scenes of *These Thousand Hills* does Lat Evans face the historical reality of that conflict. Beginning with the second section of the novel, after his initial success in Montana (when he tames a wild horse belonging to a conman named Jehu), he pursues the "chances and choices" of Montana, seemingly unaware of the contradiction between his historical role as a respectable citizen of a growing society and the unspoiled country that once opened before him. At times, he senses that he is losing something at the very moment that he is realizing his dreams of success and tries, therefore, to cling to the memories and friends of the past. Eventually, however, Lat discovers that the nostalgia that is caused by historical change is both inescapable and useless as a defense against the consequences of history.

On the cattle drive and then in Fort Benton, Lat befriends Tom Ping and Callie Kash—two characters who remain in his life yet represent, as time goes by, the openness and freedom that are rapidly receding into his past. Tom can not share Lat's visions of success; nothing is worth the sacrifice of one's independence for the pleasure of society. "You aim high, pard," he tells Lat; "You want things nice. Nice outfit somewheres. . . . [But] I don't go for swelled-up men and high-toned, dear-me ladies and stuck-up manners and houses built to mortify a common man" (p. 110). For Tom, the winter of wolfing with Lat and two others from the cattle drive is almost an end in itself; for Lat it is only a means to an end, another step toward his future ranch. And it is his eagerness to skin every wolf he can find (by first killing and poisoning the decreasing number of buffalo) that leads to his and Tom's capture by Indians, an episode that symbolizes the conflict in *These Thousand Hills* between the demands of society and a stage of frontier existence that is passing away. Tom chooses to stay with Lat throughout a long journey with their Indian captors, not escaping when he has the chance; but then, after their release (thanks to Lat's healing of a wounded brave), Tom abandons Lat in Fort Benton when Lat returns again to his dreams of becoming a respectable rancher and refuses to "stand up" with Callie Kash at Tom's marriage to another prostitute. To Tom, who has always thought of himself and Lat as "no special prizes in the grab bag" (p. 184), Lat's refusal smacks of the "swelled-up men" and "high society" that he can not stand.

Lat's choice is by no means easy, however; he is both "pious" and "pussy-struck," as Tom puts it. He had fallen in love with Callie when his future was none too bright. Though she loves him for her part and dotes upon his "spells of backwardness," she is also more willing to acknowledge the social distinctions that may separate them in the future, as, for example, in her sensitivity to the contradiction between Lat's going to his first church service in Tansytown and then seeing her afterwards (p. 245).

> She saw the great miles of this country stretching between them, the lost and impossible miles, and the miles of his interests reaching farther and farther, beyond sight, beyond all but the whisper of memory (p. 172).

Though she is "unstarched" compared to Lat's dreams of the future, Callie has her place—even a respectable place—in a certain stage of frontier society. Aunt Fran's whorehouse in Fort Benton is one of the established institutions of the town, a "regular parlor house" in a "clutch of log and 'dobe houses and rare new brick and false fronts" (pp. 66, 79). In a comical scene, Aunt Fran insists that Lat's parents would not approve of his not paying for Callie's services, since she—Aunt Fran—has "the responsibilities of a going and respectable house where the likes of him," thinks Lat, "was too low, being broke, and lower yet, being so high-minded about virtue and sin" (p. 144).

It is Callie who loans Lat the money ($1,000) to bet on himself in a race against an Indian pony, and, thereby, enables him to buy land and become, three years later, the most successful rancher in the area. But, as the horse race approaches, Callie discovers that she is out of place in Lat's thoughts,

> crowded aside, poor second to cattle and grass. He would leave her if he could, would follow his interests to parts far away and forever be lost to her except that at night now and then perhaps he'd remember and hitch over in bed, wishing he could have her or forget her in sleep (p. 171).

The more successful Lat becomes, the more conscious he is of Callie's occupation. As one of his friends observes, wryly, "it wasn't until white wives and picket fences began comin' in that a man got damned for actin' the man. . . . No one hates a whore like a cold wife unless it's the husband she won't let out of sight. So we got vice for a word" (p. 215). In Lat's case, his touchiness about the secrets of his past is attributable, in part, to the desire to fulfill the expectations of his bitterly religious father, who had never forgiven his own wife for being pregant by another man when he agreed to marry her (on the trail to Oregon in *The Way West*). When the banker who matches Lat's winnings in the horse race warns him against thinking "the business of ranching can be tended to in bars and hookshops," Lat insists that he knows better—"Evans," he says, "is a good name in Oregon" (pp. 190, 191).

For a while, after his success at ranching, Lat continues to see Callie—"out of some due and upside-down decency" (p. 191)—but insists that she treat him as a paying customer; in the end, however, he has to find a "decent way out of indecency" (p. 244). It was "his own nature," he decides, that "wanted to be good": "He wanted his life open and solid and respectable. He had always wanted . . . to be a good boy, a good man, eventually a good husband and father, and to be known as such. He was a Methodist" (p. 244). Years later, after his marriage to Joyce

Sheridan (a fellow Methodist from Indiana), Lat dreams of Callie and Tom Ping and the horse that he once tamed and rode to victory: in the dream, Lat is being chased by a hoard of black shapes (perhaps the buffalo that are by then extinct in Montana) that grow wings and merge into a giant bird, hovering over his head; in fleeing he pushes Tom Ping aside and sees Callie far in the distance on his horse. He calls to her to come back, but she rides over the edge of an abyss and disappears from sight. As he shouts her name, ears sprout from the ground like cactus, and he himself falls "in a sudden darkness cast by wings overhead" (p. 275). The significance of the dream seems to be that Lat can not escape the consequences of the historical changes that he has helped to bring about; the past remains, in memory if not in fact, to pursue him like the furies and to jeopardize the aspirations that are based on those same historical changes. Callie and Tom Ping embody the stasis of a life that Lat has left behind—a simpler, more natural existence without the moral conventions of a more complex civilization.

"You'll never live down your trainin'," one of Lat's friends tells him referring to his hospitality (p. 197). The comment applies to his attitudes as well: Lat will always dream of the future and yearn, nostalgically, for the past. The ancient buffalo bull that he finds wandering on the prairie, at the beginning of the novel's fourth section, is merely a reminder of his ambivalent historical situation. The buffalo is doomed to be killed by the wolves that are surrounding him. Lat tries to help by driving him toward his cabin, "to safety and hay," but the buffalo, in effect, refuses to be domesticated. There is nothing Lat can do but "ride on" and accept his own complicity in the events of history. The final two sections of *These Thousand Hills* recount his journey toward that acceptance.

After years of ranching, Lat's controversial ideas pay off—the owning and leasing of land, irrigation, haying, and closer herding—and establish him as the leading citizen of Tansytown, Montana, with a possible future in state politics. Thinking of his own success and his likely involvement in Montana's progress toward statehood, Lat recalls his grandfather's old words—"A man likes to grow up with the country. And when he gets growed up, he likes the country growed up, too"—and thinks that he finally understands what they meant (p. 253). The "wish of self-importance," however, has caused Lat to forget the rest of his grandfather's observation—"or maybe he does or maybe he don't. Some ways one way, some was t'other." His own success, Lat soon discovers, brings obligations of a nature he had never expected. Specifically, the cattle thieves that are victimizing those ranchers who have been more foolish and less successful than Lat force him to defend some interests other than his own. No matter how civilized the future may be that he envisions for Tansytown, he and the other ranchers must resort to frontier justice—a vigilante raid—to achieve that goal. Again, he thinks, "his course was fixed" into the future, yet somehow compromised at the same time, somehow lowered, by time itself, to the level of "rough choices" and harsh reality.

When he discovers that Tom Ping is one of the rustlers, Lat manages to sound a premature alarm that allows Tom to escape from the vicinity of the cabin where the others are trapped and killed. Lat himself catches up with Tom and, in an attempt to regain his trust, allows him to go free. He does not understand that even his kindness, in Tom's eyes, has become patronizing—another high-toned gesture. Nothing Lat does, in fact, from this point on in the novel, can alleviate the conflict between his past and present. Earlier, his maternal grandfather McBee (a disreputable pioneer in *The Way West*) had turned up out of nowhere, and Lat had bought him off with $100 and a horse; but McBee stays around town and, when Lat refuses him another cent, threatens to reveal their relationship. Instead, however, he tells Lat that his mother—McBee's daughter—"birthed a bastard . . . your older brother, him that's dead" (p. 341). To this Lat responds by throwing McBee out of the bar and, tired of his shame, finally acknowledges the old man as his grandfather.

But this is just the beginning of Lat Evans's final accounting in *These Thousand Hills*. Beside Tom Ping and McBee, Lat must also cope again with Callie Kash. When a dead man is found in her

Tansytown whorehouse, she becomes the logical suspect, and Lat is called out of his marriage bed to come to her aid. Just as Tom Ping had once asked him to stand up with Callie at Tom's wedding, Lat is asked to "stand up" as a character witness (in the event of a trial) for Callie herself. The "upside-down decency" he has always felt toward Callie causes him, this time, to agree and to risk, thereby, his own political future. Eventually, Callie leaves town and nothing comes of the entire incident, but Lat is driven by his mounting obligations to the past to tell his wife the whole story. In four years of marriage, she has never adjusted to life on the frontier, and Lat for his own part has tried "to shield and protect her, to save her from trial and hurt" (p. 311). Even after he has told her about Callie and the vigilantes and McBee, he still tries to believe that "what's past is past and doesn't matter when we love each other" (pp. 329–30). But his long attempts to keep up appearances only make the truth more painful when it eventually surfaces; and his wife locks herself in their bedroom.

Ironically, as Lat wanders purposelessly around the town, he meets Mr. Strain, the storekeeper who originally sponsored his membership in the local Methodist church and on the school board; Strain's hopeful visions suddenly have a hollow ring for Lat:

> We're changing fast, Lat. The whole country is. More and more, Joyce will come to feel at home here. . . . It takes time to civilize a new place, but we're almost there. . . . We'll have better courts, better law enforcement, more churches and schools, a more general respect and support for the finer things. . . . And you, my boy, will play a big part in the process (p. 332).

The optimism of this vision may be justified, even concerning Lat's future participation, but for the reader of *These Thousand Hills* the issue is neither so simple nor so one-sided. These changes will come, too, undoubtedly, but not, for Lat, without the pain of having to sacrifice the feelings and virtues that he would like to retain from a simpler past.

This is the import of the novel's final scenes. After Lat disposes of his grandfather McBee in the bar, he is goaded into a confrontation by Tom Ping, who deliberately provokes him with memories of their days together before Lat's success in Tansytown. Ping calls him a "one-horse rancher" and "a goddam high-winker"; "you never made good on a friendship yet," he says, referring to Lat's original refusal to risk his future reputation by appearing with Callie at Tom's wedding. Confronted with these reminders of the past, Lat finds himself, for an instant,

> beyond the dark face, behind the waiting time . . . in Fort Benton again. He had come from the bank, and Tom was heeling from him with hurt and anger in his look and on his lips a foul goodbye (p. 343).

Tom Ping stands away from the bar, ready to draw his gun; but Lat chooses to turn his back and leave. By hearing him out, "Lat had called Ping's hand," thinks a mutual friend from the days of the trail drive.

> Not that he'd had too much choice, but still he'd forced the showdown. Then something had come over him. Carmichael didn't know what. He only knew it wasn't fear. He only knew the Senate was gone sure enough then. He only knew, this above all, that Lat could have killed Ping—and didn't (p. 344).

Instead of killing Ping, Lat performs an act of courage that appears, purposely, to be an act of cowardice, thereby accepting Ping's judgment and acknowledging his own fallibility. "Senator!" someone in the bar snickers, to which Tom Ping replies, with desperate comprehension, "He's not a coward. . . . You cheap chippies, he's a better man than all of you" (p. 344).

As Lat walks out of the bar and heads home, he seems to Carmichael "a man laid bare, peeled to the bone, without explanation or apology carrying his skull on the skeleton that was left of him" (p. 344). That his wife, in the end, opens the door to him in his time of need does not alter the fact that Lat has willingly faced, for the first time in his life, the ambivalence of his own historical situation and the pain that it has caused. Such a resolution hardly represents, as James K. Folsom has charged, "a resounding affirmation of conventional values"; nor does Lat's respectable wife become the "quintessence of [his] heart's desire" to whose forgiving arms he returns, "secure in the knowledge that love conquers all."[8]

On the contrary, when Lat came to Montana, he had tried to substantiate, in his own experience, an old myth of a Promised Land, and it disappointed him as it disappointed his father before him in Oregon. The myth was tenable only as long as the open spaces and distant reaches of Montana, which he shared in the beginning with Tom Ping, remained unchanged. But the myth itself necessitated change and once again, as in Oregon, brought on the rude awakenings of history—the truth, namely, that nothing is gained in time without a commensurate loss, that one can speak of success, but never in any absolute sense. One of Guthrie's characters in *Arfive* puts it well: "Change is the order of nature. It is in our nature somehow to resist while forwarding it. What comes comes, to our dismay or delight or more likely both, and both diminished."[9] In Lat's case, the evolution of a simpler, more natural frontier society into an increasingly demanding civilization with its inescapable conventions caused a conflict between his desire for stability and permanence, represented more and more by the past, and his desire to grow up with the country. His mistake was in assuming that he could find and preserve the promised land of his dreams, despite the consequences of historical change; thus, his nostalgic need to feel morally superior to time and change only postponed his full recognition of both his own weaknesses and the mutability of history.

Like all the central characters in the foregoing novels, Lat Evans is caught in a "democratic" predicament. To be unwilling either to change with one's society or to accept the results of those changes is to deceive oneself and, perhaps, even to invite the kind of self-destruction described in *The House of Mirth, The Sheltered Life,* or *The Fathers.* If American society has been anything, these authors seem to be saying, it has been a society of change and disappointment.

Conclusion:
The Present Situation

All of the novels discussed in the preceding chapters manifest, to one degree or another, a positive structural tension, as opposed to the destructive tension between the demands of plot and the demands of characterization that one also finds in *The Pioneers* and *The House of the Seven Gables*. Again, to quote Henry James, the "consciousness of the complication exhibited," on the part of the central characters in these novels, "forms for us their link of connection with it." That tension between objective events—a changing physical and social environment—and the individual's subjective awareness of those events provides the best measure of the success or failure of these novels as works of art. Only when this relationship is weighted in one direction or the other is the novel weakened. This is the case, one could argue, in Adams's *Democracy* and Wharton's *The House of Mirth*, that might well have benefited from less description of surface manners and more development of the attitudes that demand an adherence to those manners. Similarly, there are moments in *The Professor's House* (St. Peter's loss of control in book 3), *The Fathers* (the immediate events leading up to the murders of Yellow Jim and Semmes), and *These Thousand Hills* (Lat Evans's confrontation with Tom Ping and his wife's final fogiveness) when a dramatic crisis provokes an increase in the rapidity of action and a commensurate decrease in the clarity of character motivation. Thus the urgency of a fictional situation is reflected in a misplaced urgency of style.

On the other hand, the consciousness of characters in these novels can also become dominant, thereby retarding unnecessarily the story's tempo. Witness, for example, the concentrated introspection of General Archbald in the second section of *The Sheltered Life,* which finally confuses the issues of the novel no matter how lyrical the passage may seem by itself. In the last analysis, *The Bostonians* and *The Hamlet* are probably the best of the novels discussed here principally because they come closest to achieving the right tension between events and their characters' consciousness of events. In James, that consciousness is far more explicit than it is in the case of Faulkner's farmers; but, articulated or not, the intense awareness of and opposition to Flem Snopes's presence in Frenchman's Bend is still there in *The Hamlet.* If Faulkner's characters could have more clearly identified their enemy and directed their efforts against him rather than themselves, their resistance to change, however fruitless, would have appeared more explicit to the reader.

In short, to project a sense of the tension between an inevitable process of social change and the nostalgia that envisions a "better" time in the past, the novelist must find the right formal balance between external events and the implicit or explicit awareness of those events. It must be a balance, in effect, between an author's loyalty to the depiction of a particular social context and his sympathy for the universal desire to escape its harsher restrictions.

This sensibility—the acute awareness of the tension between inevitable social change and the individual's yearning for permanence and harmony—seems now to be less apparent than it used to be in the American novel. Perhaps one could argue that a true sense of social change can not operate without the consciousness of a somewhat identifiable, established background against which to measure the forces and momentum of history. In any event, this concern seems to have been superseded for many American writers by a sense of social alienation and absurdity, according to which any "once familiar social categories and placemarks," in Irving Howe's words, "have now become as uncertain and elusive as the moral imperatives of the nineteenth century seemed to novelists of fifty years ago." Howe has called this newest social situation the "mass society" and listed as one of its general characteristics the heightened obscuration of class differences and the breakdown of "traditional centers of authority, like the family." Above all, despite the greater affluence of the mass society, the individual has become "increasingly aware of [his] social dependence and powerlessness." Since the Second World War, Howe argued, American society has not lent itself as well to "assured definition" and the novelist "could no longer assume as quickly as in the recent past that a spiritual or moral difficulty could find a precise embodiment in a social conflict,"[1] as it did in the conflict discussed here between social change and nostalgia. Consequently, the hero of the contemporary American novel, from Salinger and Ellison to Heller and Donleavy, often appears in the guise of an antihero, alienated from any and all manifestations of society. Nor is this absence of any "mediation between Self and World," as Ihab Hassan has put it,[2] without precedents in the American novel: Captain Ahab and Huck Finn, among others, can testify to this fact. Wherever it has appeared, such alienation has been absolute and has not been, itself, the product of history and the passage of time.

All of this notwithstanding, the past still exists, for any society, whether it is recognized or not. Put another way, a given culture never loses its past, only what Wallace Stegner has called its "sense of a personal and *possessed* past."[3] And, in Stegner's view,

> if you are any part of an artist, and a lot of people are some part of one, if you have any desire to understand, and thus to help steer, a civilization that seems to have got away from us, then I think you don't choose between the past and the present; you try to find the connections, you try to make the one serve the other.[4]

If nostalgia and "disgust for the shoddy present" is not enough, in such circumstances, then it is also true that forgetting the past entirely is "a dehumanizing error."[5]

From Cooper to Faulkner and beyond, some of the best novelists in America have refused either to forget the past or to give in to a tempting nostalgia. The works discussed here represent, in effect, a minor tradition of the nonhero, as opposed to the ubiquitous antihero of the contemporary novel. While the traditional hero in American fiction, as well as his opposite number, the antihero, have both been distinguished from society at large, either in transcendence or in alienation, those novels that deal with the nonhero find the "Self" inseparable from his "World." Though such characters experience a form of alienation, it is an alienation, not of self from world, but of one world from another in the continuity of time.

Perhaps some critics of American literature, in their nerverending search for what distinguishes American literature from other national literatures, ought to look in this direction. It often seems, in fact, that scholars are determined to find a *distinctive* tradition in American fiction that is also the *dominant* tradition. And, in so doing, they appear bent upon reenacting the very love of freedom and escape that has been repeatedly attributed to the American novelist and his heroes. To apply a statement by Richard Poirier to scholarly research, American critics, like their alter egos—the writer and his hero—tend to want "to believe, repetitively, despite history and their own experience, in the transcendental power of their own stylistic enterprise."[6] Thus, just as the American hero's identity, according to some critics, lies in his freedom from social entanglements, the identity of the American novel must lie in the autonomy of its form and style.

But, in reality, American society and American literature, much as one might hate to admit it, probably have more in common than in conflict with other Western societies and literatures. It would be good for all scholars who profess to appreciate American literature to consider that what is most distinctive about American fiction may be far from dominant, and may itself represent merely a difference in degree, rather than kind, from other literatures. In doing so, one may discover, as Norman Mailer has suggested in describing the "muted tragedy of the Wasp" in America, a real discrepancy between what is dominant and what is most distinctive in our society. Specifically, Mailer concludes (in *Miami and the Seige of Chicago*) that those

Americans who were the economic, family, military, and "spiritual" power of the country were not, finally, as powerful as history itself:

> they were not on earth to enjoy or even perhaps to love so very much, they were here to serve, and serve they had in public functions and public charities (while recipients of their charity might vomit in rage and laugh in scorn), served on opera committees, and served in long hours of duty at the piano, served as the sentinel in concert halls and the pews on the aisle in church, at the desk in schools, had served for culture, served for finance, served for salvation, served for America—and so much of America did not wish them to serve any longer, and so many of them doubted themselves, doubted that the force of their faith could illumine their path in these new modern horror-head times.... Now they were looking for a leader to bring America back to them, their lost America, Jesus-land.[7]

Here, in a contemporary setting, an American writer presents his readers with a dramatic situation very similar to those found in the novels discussed in this study of American fiction. Such a situation, however limited it has been in the frequency of its appearance (as distinguished from its perseverance), may well be as characteristically American as any situation in the American novel. At its heart lies the basic assumption that the reality of American society—past, present, and the connection between the two—has been its essential impermanence.

A final word needs to be said about the "racial" nature of this literary phenomenon, since it is difficult to imagine a novel like those discussed here having been written by a Negro, an American Indian, or a member of any other distinctive minority culture in the United States. The "sense of the sense of the past" of white writers, since the inception of American fiction, is still, despite its fundamental honesty, a characteristic vision of history for those who have never had an enduring past of their own. Progress after all, with its consequent inescapable changes in society, has been a white man's invention in America and, psychologically, the white man's burden. Here, the central contrast in Willa Cather's *Death Comes for the Archbishop* is illustrative:

When they left the rock or tree or sand dune that had sheltered them for the night, the Navajo was careful to obliterate
every trace of their temporary occupation. He buried the em-
bers of the fire and the remnants of food, unpiled any stones
he had piled together, filled up the holes he had scooped in
the sand. Since this was exactly Jacinto's procedure, Father
Latour judged that, just as it was the white man's way to assert
himself in any landscape, to change it, make it over a little (at
least to leave some mark or memorial of his sojourn), it was the
Indian's way to pass through a country without disturbing
anything; to pass and leave no trace, like fish through the
water, or birds through the air.[8]

Similarly, the persistent nostalgia of a recent novel like N. Scott
Momaday's *House Made of Dawn* does not, in the end, seem self-
delusive. In the aftermath and backwash of military service and
urban immersion, the young Indian in that novel can and must
go home again; the land is always there, and his past need never,
finally, be past.

Though Black Americans have not had the "eternal" resources
of Indian culture, they have seldom been, on the other hand, in
a position in which social change has seemed a regrettable thing;
there is no possibility of nostalgia, for example, in *Native Son*.
Perhaps if whites can realize the self-inflicted nature of their
historical burdens—namely, the rapidly altering society to
which they pay their allegiance—then they may be able to heigh-
ten their appreciation of those Americans for whom nostalgia
has been either fruitful or impossible, rather than a matter of
continual anxiety and frustration. They might, at long last, begin
to view themselves and their past realistically.

Notes

Introduction

1. Eleanor N. Hutchens, "The Novel as Chronomorph," *Novel* 5 (1972): 219–20, 222.

2. *See,* in particular, William Bradford, *Of Plymouth Plantation,* ed. Samuel Eliot Morison (New York: Alfred A. Knopf, 1963), pp. 253–54; Alexis de Tocqueville, *Democracy in America,* ed. Phillips Bradley, 2 vols. (New York: Alfred A. Knopf, 1945), 1: 249; R. W. Emerson, *The Heart of Emerson's Journals,* ed. Bliss Perry (New York: Dover, 1958), p. 260; Charles Dickens, *American Notes for General Circulation,* ("Postscript") (New York: Scribner's, 1910), p. 303; and C. E. Norton, *Letters of Charles Eliot Norton,* ed. Sara Norton and M. A. DeWolfe Howe, 2 vols. (Boston: Houghton Mifflin, 1913), 2: 244.

3. de Tocqueville, 2: 239.

4. Richard Chase, *The American Novel and Its Tradition* (Garden City, New York: Doubleday, 1957), p. 159.

5. Marius Bewley, *The Eccentric Design: Form in the Classic American Novel* (New York: Columbia University Press, 1957), p. 15. *See also* Lionel Trilling, *The Liberal Imagination,* ("Manners, Morals, and the Novel") (Garden City, New York: Doubleday, 1950), pp. 205–22, and Joel Porte, *The Romance in America* (Middletown, Connecticut: Wesleyan University Press, 1969).

6. A notable exception is a recent article by Nicolaus Mills, "American Fiction and the Genre Critics," *Novel* 2 (1969): 112–22.

7. Irving Howe, "Mass Society and Post-Modern Fiction," *Partisan Review* 26 (1959): 425.

8. L. Trilling, "Art and Fortune," p. 252.

9. de Tocqueville, 2: 105.

10. Henry James, *The Art of the Novel,* preface to *The Princess Casamassima,* ed. R. P. Blackmur (New York: Scribner's, 1934), p. 62.

11. This is what distinguishes Lily Bart's situation in *The House of*

Mirth, for example, from the less reflective and explicit situations of the central characters in other urban novels that focus on the capriciousness of change (such as Theodore Dreiser's *Sister Carrie* or Saul Bellow's *Seize the Day*).

12. C. G. Jung, *Modern Man in Search of a Soul,* trans. W. S. Dell and Cary F. Baynes (New York: Harcourt, Brace and World, 1933), p. 217.

13. Ibid., p. 220.

14. As opposed to the authorial nostalgia that dominates such novels as Cooper's *The Deerslayer,* Twain's *The Adventures of Tom Sawyer,* Cather's *My Ántonia,* and Sherwood Anderson's *Poor White.*

15. Henry Adams, *Democracy* (New York: Henry Holt and Company, 1880), p. 144.

16. Henry James, *The Bostonians* (New York: Macmillan and Co., 1886), pp. 189–90.

17. Ellen Glasgow, *The Sheltered Life* (Garden City, New York: Doubleday, Doran, 1934), p. 144.

18. Andrew Wright, *Jane Austen's Novels: A Study in Structure* (New York: Oxford University Press, 1961), pp. 24, 28.

19. Ibid., p. 26.

20. Nicholas Berdyaev, *The Meaning of History,* trans. Geoge Reavey (Cleveland, Ohio: World, 1962), p. 16.

21. de Tocqueville, 2: 145.

22. James Fenimore Cooper, *Home as Found* (New York: Putnam's, 1912), p. 4.

23. Nathaniel Hawthorne, *The Complete Novels and Selected Tales of Nathaniel Hawthorne,* ed. Norman Holmes Pearson (New York: Random House, 1937), p. 590.

24. T. S. Eliot, "The Hawthorne Aspect," in *The Shock of Recognition,* ed. Edmund Wilson (New York: Farrar, Straus, and Cudahy, 1955), p. 861.

1

1. James Fenimore Cooper, *The Spy* (Philadelphia: Carey, Lea, and Blanchard, 1836), p. 7.

2. J. F. Cooper, *Home as Found,* pp. 3–4.

3. James Fenimore Cooper, *Notions of the Americans: Picked Up by a Travelling Bachelor,* 2 vols. (Philadelphia: Carey, Lea, and Carey, 1828), 2: 108.

4. James Fenimore Cooper, *Satanstoe* (New York: Putnam's, 1912), p. 3.

5. James Fenimore Cooper, *The Pioneers* (New York: Holt, Rinehart, and Winston, 1959), p. 26.

6. Donald Davie, *The Heyday of Sir Walter Scott* (London: Routledge and Kegan Paul, 1961), p. 130.

7. Ibid.

8. D. H. Lawrence, *Studies in Classic American Literature* (New York: Viking, 1964), p. 52.

9. Ibid., p. 50.

10. D. Davie, p. 127.

11. James Fenimore Cooper, *The Deerslayer* (New York: Putnam's, 1912), p. 46. Future page numbers will follow quotations.

12. James Fenimore Cooper, *The Pioneers* (New York: Putnam's, 1912), p. 423. Hereafter, all quotations from this edition will be followed directly by their page numbers.

13. J. F. Cooper, *The Pioneers* (New York: Holt, Rinehart, and Winston, 1959), p. 26.

14. These are Mr. Davie's terms. His argument that the central issue of *The Pioneers* is "freedom vs anarchy," not "freedom vs law" (p. 143), is interesting, but the distinction is irrelevant for Natty, who sees quite clearly that human law will always permit and protect that depredation that benefits the social community.

15. Thomas Philbrick's contention that Natty Bumppo, in *The Pioneers*, "rejects the very idea of a human community" is unfortunate: "he is the advocate of animals and trees and the enemy of man and human values." To make this kind of statement is to misrepresent the moral impulse behind Natty's position. He rejects the particular human community that Marmaduke Temple fosters and absolves, which can not be equated with "human values" in general. "Cooper's *The Pioneers*: Origins and Structure," *PMLA* 79 (1964): 591–92.

16. T. Philbrick, p. 592. "He is heir to a long tradition of honor, of loyalty to established authority, of continuity in religion and social class. The Effingham line has been a race of soldiers and is distinguished by its chivalric idealism and its absolute integrity, qualities that contrast sharply with the shrewdness, flexibility, and expediency of the mercantile world in which Marmaduke Temple has been schooled."

17. James Fenimore Cooper, *The American Democrat* (New York: Alfred A. Knopf, 1931), p. 75.

18. Howard Mumford Jones, *The Pursuit of Happiness* (Cambridge Massachusetts: Harvard University Press, 1953), p. 109.

19. J. F. Cooper, *The American Democrat*, p. 86.

2

1. Nathaniel Hawthorne, *The Complete Novels and Selected Tales*, p. 243. Hereafter, all quotations from this edition will be followed directly by their page numbers.

2. Henry James, "Nathaniel Hawthorne," in *Library of the World's Best Literature*, ed. Charles Dudley Warner, 31 vols. (New York: R. S. Peale and J. A. Hill, 1897), 12: 7, 053–54.

3. John Stubbs's contention that the cent-shop scenes are a "parody" of Pyncheon pride must be qualified by the fact that Hepzibah's pride is so harmless compared to that of her family in the past. *The Pursuit of Forms: A Study of Nathaniel Hawthorn and the Romance* (Champaign, Ill.: University of Illinois Press, 1970), pp. 107–08.

4. H. James, *Hawthorne* (Ithaca, N.Y.: Cornell University Press,) p. 102.

5. H. James, "Nathaniel Hawthorne," p. 7,057.

6. de Tocqueville, 2: 107.

3

1. Henry David Aiken, Foreward, *Democracy* (New York: The New American Library, 1961), p. 10.

2. Henry Adams, *The Education of Henry Adams* (New York: Random House, 1931), pp. 301, 460.

3. Henry Adams, *Democracy* (New York: Henry Holt and Company, 1880), p. 10. Hereafter, all quotations from this edition will be followed directly by their page numbers.

4. de Tocqueville, 2: 239.

5. R. P. Blackmur, "The Novels of Henry Adams," *The Sewanee Review* 50 (1943): 294.

4

1. *The Bostonians* is most often compared to Nathaniel Hawthorne's *The Blithedale Romance* in characterization and theme; but the issues raised in the following discussion of the novel suggest, I think, that *The Bostonians* is ultimately different from *The Blithedale Romance* for the same reason that it is similar to *The House of the Seven Gables:* it presents its characters as bound more by time than by human nature. For a recent comparison of *The Bostonians* and *The Blithedale Romance, see* R. E. Long, "The Society and the Masks: *The Blithedale Romance* and *The Bostonians," Nineteenth-Century Fiction* 19 (1964): 105–22.

2. Irving Howe, Introduction to H. James's *The Bostonians* (New York: Random House, 1956), p. 6.

3. Henry James, "Ivan Turgenev," in *Library of the World's Best Literature,* ed. Charles Dudley Warner, 31 vols., (New York: R. S. Reale and J. A. Hill, 1897), 25: 15,06l.

4. Henry James, *The Bostonians* (New York: Macmillan, 1886), pp. 189–90. Hereafter, all quotations from this edition will be followed directly by their page numbers.

5. Henry James, *The Notebooks of Henry James*, ed. F. O. Matthiessen and Kenneth B. Murdock (New York: Oxford University Press, 1947), p. 47.

6. I. Howe, Introduction, p. 15.

7. L. Trilling, "Manners, Morals, and the Novel," p. 203.

8. I. Howe, Introduction, p. 28.

5

1. Edith Wharton, *The House of Mirth* (New York: Charles Scribner's Sons, 1905), p. 144. Hereafter, all quotations from this edition will be followed directly by their page numbers.

2. de Tocqueville, 2: 105.

3. Ibid., 2: 239–40.

4. Edith Wharton, *The Custom of the Country* (New York: Scribner's, 1913), p. 280.

5. Louis Auchincloss, *Edith Wharton* (Minneapolis, Minnesota: University of Minnesota Press, 1961), p. 13.

6. de Tocqueville, 2: 229.

6

1. Alfred Kazin, *On Native Grounds: An Interpretation of Modern American Prose Literature* (Garden City, New York: Doubleday, 1956), p. 188.

2. Willa Cather, *The Professor's House* (New York: Alfred A. Knopf, 1925), p. 258. Hereafter, all quotations from this edition will be followed directly by their page numbers.

3. Leon Edel, *Literary Biography* (Toronto, Canada: University of Toronto Press, 1957), pp. 78–79. Edel limits the list of available reasons for St. Peter's depression to "the materialism of an age, the marrying off of one's children to persons we may like or dislike, [and] the process of growing old."

4. Edward and Lillian Bloom, *Willa Cather's Gift of Sympathy* (Carbondale, Ill.: Southern Illinois University Press, 1962), p. 113.

5. Sherwood Anderson, *The Portable Sherwood Anderson*, ed. Horace Gregory (New York: Viking, 1949), p. 548.

7

1. Including A. Kazin, *On Native Grounds,* p. 195; Frederick P. W. McDowell, *Ellen Glasgow and the Ironic Art of fiction* (Madison, Wis.: University of Wisconsin Press, 1960), p. 201; and Blair Rouse, *Ellen Glasgow* (New York: Twayne, 1962), p. 108.

2. Ellen Glasgow, *Letters of Ellen Glasgow,* ed. Blair Rouse (New York: Harcourt, Brace, 1958), p. 206.

3. Ibid., p. 342.

4. Ellen Glasgow, *The Sheltered Life,* p. 377. Hereafter, all quotations from this edition will be followed directly by their page numbers.

5. A. Kazin, p. 193.

6. Ibid.

7. Louis Auchincloss, *Ellen Glasgow* (Minneapolis, Minnesota: University of Minnesota Press, 1964), p. 32.

8. E. Glasgow, *Letters,* p. 122.

9. Ibid., p. 124.

8

1. Arthur Mizener, "The Fathers," *The Sewane Review* 67 (1959): 606.

2. Allen Tate, *The Fathers* (New York: G. P. Putnam's Sons, 1938), p. 178. Hereafter, all quotations from this edition will be followed directly by their page numbers.

9

1. R. Chase, p. 158.

2. Ibid., p. 231.

3. William Faulkner, *The Hamlet* (New York: Random House, 1940), pp. 65–66. Hereafter, all quotations from this edition will be followed directly by their page numbers.

4. Olga Vickery, *The Novels of William Faulkner* (Baton Rouge, LA.: Louisiana State University Press, 1959), p. 171.

5. Irving Howe, *William Faulkner: A Critical Study* (New York: Alfred A. Knopf, 1962), p. 289.

6. James Gray Watson's assertion that Flem Snopes's successes in Frenchman's Bend, though inevitable, are "self-annihilating" and that "the rejuvenatory nature of the moral world is revealed in the temporariness of its defeats" is an imposition of further developments in *The Town* and *The Mansion* on the text of *The Hamlet.* It is more accurate to say, with Richard P. Adams, that *The Hamlet,* at best, affirms the

"going on" quality of life. *See* Watson, *The Snopes Dilemma: Faulkner's Trilogy* (Coral Gables, Florida: University of Miami Press, 1968), p. 18; and Adams, *Faulkner: Myth and Motion,* (Princeton, N.J.: Princeton University Press, 1968), pp. 119–20.

7. Irving Howe, "William Faulkner," in *Major Writers of America,* 2 vols., ed. P. Miller (New York: Harcourt, Brace and World, 1962), 2: 841.

8. I. Howe, *William Faulkner,* p. 287.

10

1. A. B. Guthrie, Jr., *The Way West* (New York: William Sloane, 1949), p. 217.

2. Wallace Stegner, *The Sound of Mountain Water* (New York: Doubleday, 1969), p. 256.

3. A. B. Guthrie, Jr., *The Blue Hen's Chick* (New York: McGraw-Hill, 1965), p. 251.

4. W. Stegner, p. 257.

5. A. B. Guthrie, Jr., *The Big Sky* (New York: William Sloane, 1947), p. 211.

6. A. B. Guthrie, Jr., *The Way West,* p. 280.

7. A. B. Guthrie, Jr., *These Thousand Hills* (Boston: Houghton Mifflin, 1956), pp. 187–88. Hereafter, all quotations from this edition will be followed directly by their page numbers.

8. James K. Folsom, *The American Western Novel* (New Haven, Connecticut: College and University Press, 1966), p. 74.

9. A. B. Guthrie, Jr., *Arfive* (Boston: Houghton Mifflin, 1971), p. 101.

Conclusion

1. I. Howe, "Mass Society and Post-Modern Fiction," pp. 426–28.

2. Ihab Hassan, *Radical Innocence: Studies in the Contemporary American Novel* (Princeton, N.J.: Princeton University Press, 1961), p.327.

3. W. Stegner, p. 199.

4. Ibid., p. 200.

5. Ibid., p. 199.

6. Richard Poirier, *A World Elsewhere: The Place of Style in American Literature* (New York: Oxford University Press, 1966), p. 17.

7. Norman Mailer, *Miami and the Seige of Chicago* (New York: The New American Library, 1968), pp. 35–36.

8. Willa Cather, *Death Comes for the Archbishop* (New York: Alfred A. Knopf, 1927), p. 233.

Selected Bibliography

Adams, Henry. *Democracy*. New York: Henry Holt and Company, 1880.

———. *The Education of Henry Adams*. New York: Random House, 1931.

———. *Esther*. New York: Henry Holt and Company, 1884.

Adams, Richard P. *Faulkner: Myth and Motion*. Princeton, New Jersey: Princeton University Press, 1968.

Aiken, Henry David. Forward to *Democracy,* by Henry Adams. New York: The New American Library, 1961.

Anderson, Sherwood. *The Portable Sherwood Anderson*. Edited by Horace Gregory. New York: Viking, 1949.

Auchincloss, Louis. *Edith Wharton*. Minneapolis: University of Minnesota Press, 1961.

———. *Ellen Glasgow*. Minneapolis: University of Minnesota Press, 1964.

———. *Pioneers and Caretakers: A Study of Nine American Women Novelists*. Minneapolis: University of Minnesota Press, 1965.

Berdyaev, Nicholas. *The Meaning of History*. Translated by George Reavey. Cleveland, Ohio: World, 1962.

Bewley, Marius. *The Complex Fate: Hawthorne, Henry James, and Some Other American Writers*. London: Chatto and Windus, 1952.

———. *The Eccentric Design: Form in the Classic American Novel*. New York: Columbia University Press, 1957.

184

Blackmur, R. P. "The Novels of Henry Adams." *The Sewanee Review* 50:281–304.

Bloom, Edward and Lillian. *Willa Cather's Gift of Sympathy.* Carbondale, Illinois: Southern Illinois University Press, 1962.

Bradford, William. *Of Plymouth Plantation.* Edited by Samuel Eliot Morison. New York: Alfred A. Knopf, 1963.

Cather, Willa. *Death Comes for the Archbishop.* New York: Alfred A. Knopf, 1927.

———. *My Ántonia.* Boston: Houghton Mifflin, 1918.

———. *O Pioneers!* Boston: Houghton Mifflin, 1913.

———. *The Professor's House.* New York: Alfred A. Knopf, 1925.

Chase, Richard. *The American Novel and Its Tradition.* Garden City, New York: Doubleday, 1957.

Cooper, James Fenimore. *The American Democrat.* New York: Alfred A. Knopf, 1931.

———. *The Deerslayer.* New York: Putnam's, 1912.

———. *Home as Found.* New York: Putnam's, 1912.

———. *The Last of the Mohicans.* New York: Putnam's, 1912.

———. *Notions of the Americans: Picked Up by a Travelling Bachelor.* 2 vols. Philadelphia: Carey, Lea, and Carey, 1828.

———. *The Pathfinder.* New York: Putnam's, 1912.

———. *The Pioneers.* New York: Putnam's, 1912.

———. *The Pioneers.* New York: Holt, Rinehart, and Winston, 1959.

———. *The Prairie.* New York: Putnam's, 1912.

———. *Satanstoe.* New York: Putnam's, 1912.

———. *The Spy.* Philadelphia: Carey, Lea, and Blanchard, 1836.

Davie, Donald. *The Heyday of Sir Walter Scott.* London: Routledge and Kegan Paul, 1961.

Dickens, Charles. *American Notes for General Circulation.* New York: Scribner's, 1910.

Edel, Leon. *Literary Biography.* Toronto: University of Toronto Press, 1957.

Emerson, Ralph Waldo. *The Heart of Emerson's Journals.* Edited by Bliss Perry. New York: Dover, 1958.

Faulkner, William. *The Hamlet.* New York: Random House, 1940.

———. *The Mansion.* New York: Random House, 1959.

———. *The Sound and the Fury.* New York: Cape and Smith, 1929.

———. *The Town.* New York: Random House, 1957.

Feidelson, Charles, Jr. *Symbolism and American Literature.* Chicago: University of Chicago Press, 1953.

Fiedler, Leslie. *Love and Death in the American Novel.* 2d rev. ed. New York: Dell, 1966.

Folsom, James K. *The American Western Novel.* New Haven, Connecticut: College and University Press, 1966.

Fussell, Edwin. *Frontier: American Literature and the American West.* Princeton, New Jersey: Princeton University Press, 1961.

Glasgow, Ellen. *Barren Ground.* Garden City, New York: Doubleday, Page, 1925.

———. *In This Our Life.* New York: Harcourt, Brace, 1941.

———. *Letters of Ellen Glasgow.* Edited by Blair Rouse. New York: Harcourt, Brace, 1958.

———. *The Romantic Comedians.* Garden City, New York: Doubleday, Page, 1926.

———. *The Sheltered Life.* Garden City, New York: Doubleday, Doran, 1934.

———. *They Stooped to Folly.* Garden City, New York: Doubleday, Doran, 1929.

———. *Vein of Iron.* New York: Harcourt, Brace, 1935.

Guthrie, A. B., Jr. *Arfive.* Boston: Houghton Mifflin, 1971.

———. *The Big Sky.* New York: William Sloane, 1947.

———. *The Blue Hen's Chick.* New York: McGraw-Hill, 1965.

———. *These Thousand Hills.* Boston: Houghton Mifflin, 1956.

———. *The Way West.* New York: William Sloane, 1949.

Hassan, Ihab. *Radical Innocence: Studies in the Contemporary American Novel.* Princeton, New Jersey: Princeton University Press, 1961.

Hawthorne, Nathaniel. *The Complete Novels and Selected Tales of Nathaniel Hawthorne.* Edited by Norman Holmes Pearson. New York: Random House, 1937.

Hoffman, Daniel. *Form and Fable in American Literature.* New York: Oxford University Press, 1961.

Hoffman, Frederick J. *The Modern Novel in America, 1900 –1950.* 2d rev. ed. Chicago: Regnery, 1964.

Howe, Irving. Introduction to *The Bostonians,* by Henry James. New York: Random House, 1956.

———. "Mass Society and Post-Modern Fiction." *Partisan Review* 26: 420–36.

———. *William Faulkner: A Critical Study.* New York: Alfred A. Knopf, 1962.

Hutchens, Eleanor N. "The Novel as Chronomorph." *Novel* 5: 215–24.

James, Henry. *The Art of the Novel.* Edited by R. P. Blackmur. New York: Scribner's, 1934.

———. *The Bostonians.* New York: Macmillan and Co., 1886.

———. *Hawthorne.* Ithaca, New York: Cornell University Press, 1966.

———. *The Notebooks of Henry James.* Edited by F. O. Matthiessen and Kenneth B. Murdock. New York: Oxford University Press, 1947.

Jones, Howard Mumford. *The Pursuit of Happiness.* Cambridge, Massachusetts: Harvard University Press, 1953.

———. *The Theory of American Literature.* Ithaca, New York: Cornell University Press, 1948.

Jung, C. G. *Modern Man in Search of a Soul.* Translated by W. S. Dell and Cary F. Baynes. New York: Harcourt, Brace and World, 1933.

Kaul, A. N. *The American Vision: Actual and Ideal Society in Nineteenth-Century Fiction.* New Haven, Connecticut: Yale University Press, 1963.

Kazin, Alfred. *On Native Grounds: An Interpretation of Modern American Prose Literature.* Garden City, New York: Doubleday, 1956.

Lawrence, D. H. *Studies in Classic American Literature.* New York: Viking, 1964.

Lee, Robert Edson. *From West to East: Studies in the Literature of the American West.* Urbana, Illinois: University of Illinois Press, 1966.

Lewis, R. W. B. *The American Adam: Innocence, Tragedy, and Tradition in the Nineteenth Century.* Chicago: University of Chicago Press, 1955.

Long, R. E. "The Society and the Masks: *The Blithedale Romance* and *The Bostonians.*" *Nineteenth-Century Fiction* 19: 205–11.

Mailer, Norman. *Miami and the Seige of Chicago.* New York: The New American Library, 1968.

Martin, Jay. *Harvests of Change: American Literature, 1965–1914.* Englewood Cliffs, New Jersey: Prentice-Hall, 1967.

Matthiessen, F. O. *American Renaissance: Art and Expression in the Age of Emerson and Whitman.* New York: Oxford University Press, 1941.

McDowell, Frederick P. W. *Ellen Glasgow and the Ironic Art of Fiction.* Madison, Wisconsin: University of Wisconsin Press, 1960.

Miller, Perry, ed. *Major Writers of America.* 2 vols. New York: Harcourt, Brace and World, 1962.

Mills, Nicolaus. *American and English Fiction in the Nineteenth Century.* Bloomington, Indiana: Indiana University Press, 1973.

———. "American Fiction and the Genre Critics." *Novel* 2: 112–22.

Mizener, Arthur. "The Fathers." *The Sewanee Review* 67: 604–13.

Noble, David. *The Eternal Adam and the New World Garden.* New York: Braziller, 1968.

Norton, Charles Eliot. *Letters of Charles Eliot Norton.* Edited by Sara Norton and M. A. DeWolfe Howe. 2 vols. Boston: Houghton Mifflin, 1913.

Parrington, V. L. *The Romantic Revolution in America, 1800–1860.* Vol. 2 of *Main Currents in American Thought.* New York: Harcourt, Brace, 1927.

————. *The Beginnings of Critical Realism in America, 1860–1920.* Vol. 3 of *Main Currents in American Thought.* New York: Harcourt, Brace, 1930.

Philbrick, Thomas. "Cooper's *The Pioneers:* Origins and Structure." *PMLA* 79: 579–93.

Poirier, Richard. *A World Elsewhere: The Place of Style in American Literature.* New York: Oxford University Press, 1966.

Porte, Joel. *The Romance in America.* Middletown, Connecticut: Wesleyan University Press, 1969.

Rahv. *The Myth and the Powerhouse: Essays on Literature and Ideas.* New York: Farrar, Straus and Giroux, 1965.

Rourke, Constance. *American Humor.* New York: Harcourt, Brace, 1931.

Shapiro, Charles, ed. *Twelve Original Essays on Great American Novels.* Detroit, Michigan: Wayne State University Press, 1958.

Stegner, Wallace. *The Sound of Mountain Water.* New York: Doubleday, 1969.

Stubbs, John. *The Pursuit of Form: A Study of Nathaniel Hawthorne and the Romance.* Urbana, Illinois: University of Illinois Press, 1970.

Tanner, Tony. *The Reign of Wonder: Naivety and Reality in American Literature.* Cambridge (England): Cambridge University Press, 1965.

Tate, Allen. *The Fathers.* New York: Putnam's, 1938.

de Tocqueville, Alexis. *Democracy in America.* Edited by Phillips Bradley. 2 vols. New York: Alfred A. Knopf, 1945.

Trilling, Lionel. *The Liberal Imagination.* Garden City, New York: Doubleday, 1950.

Vickery, Olga. *The Novels of William Faulkner.* Baton Rouge, Louisiana: Louisiana State University Press, 1959.

Warner, Charles Dudley, ed. *Library of the World's Best Literature.* 31 vols. New York: R. S. Peale and J. A. Hill, 1897.

Watson, James Gray. *The Snopes Dilemma: Faulkner's Trilogy.* Coral Gables, Florida: University of Miami Press, 1968.

Wharton, Edith. *The Custom of the Country.* New York: Scribner's, 1913.

––––––. *The House of Mirth.* New York: Scribner's, 1905.

Wilson, Edmund, ed. *The Shock of Recognition.* New York: Farrar, Straus, and Cudahy, 1955.

Winters, Ivor. *In Defense of Reason.* New York: Swallow, 1947.

Wright, Andrew. *Jane Austen's Novels: A Study in Structure.* New York: Oxford University Press, 1961.

Author Index

191